Dining In—New Orleans
COOKBOOK

A Collection of Gourmet Recipes for Complete Meals
from the New Orleans Area's Finest Restaurants

PHYLLIS DENNERY

Foreword by
PETE FOUNTAIN

Peanut Butter Publishing
Seattle, Washington

Editor: Elaine Lotzkar
Photography & Design: Christopher Conrad
Styling & Design: Charmaine Eads
Photographer's and Stylist's Assistant: Ann White
Production: Sue Irwin
Illustration: Kelly M. Steele
Typesetting: Angus McGill, Julie Lloyd

First Printing Nov. 85
Second Printing Feb. 86
Third Printing Aug. 86
Fourth Printing Jan. 87

CONTENTS

TITLES IN SERIES

DINING IN—NEW ORLEANS
By Phyllis Dennery

Wine is an integral part of dining, and the Honorable Lindy Boggs, my representative in Congress, tells a beautiful story about why people touch wine glasses during a toast.

When one drinks wine, a Greek ship captain told Lindy, one uses his sense of touch as he embraces his glass, his sense of sight as he studies the color, his sense of taste as he rolls the wine over his tongue, his sense of smell as he whiffs the aroma—but his sense of hearing is overlooked, and his ears—they are offended! So—we clink the glasses!!

Our restaurateurs and chefs have suggested wines for most of the menus.

ACKNOWLEDGEMENTS

TO:

My Husband, Moïse —"Thank you."

Reba Lombardino —"The typist of my life."

Ula Bea Lewis —"A great tester and taster."

Victor Foster —"The best general factotum there is."

Peanut Butter Publishing Company, for all of its assistance.

And friends galore.

...

INTRODUCTION

Visitors soon learn that there are three principal topics of discussion in New Orleans—Food, Food, and Food!!!

Recent years have witnessed a quantum leap in the quality of cuisine in America. Nowhere is this *quality* more apparent than in the Cajun, the Creole, the French, the Italian, the soul food, and the Continental preparations of the imaginative and unbelievably proficient chefs of New Orleans. These chefs and our justly famous restaurants have combined to give recognition to New Orleans as the food capital of the United States.

Anyone who accepts the responsibility of selecting the top 21 restaurants in New Orleans must be a very brave or an extremely reckless person. To prove to myself that I fit in the first category, I requested six of my connoisseur (gourmet) friends to prepare a list of their favorite 21 establishments. All six lists were remarkably similar to mine.

As in most cities, restaurants are owned by chefs, business entrepreneurs, or absentee investors. In the case of these 21 restaurants, it is interesting to learn that each owner is a local resident, with his restaurant being his principal interest, and in some cases, the owner serves as the executive chef. The proprietor's attention to supervision and detail is a full-time career, which seems to have a direct relationship to the number of stars the establishment merits.

The proprietors and the chefs in New Orleans make it a practice to purchase fresh foods grown in the area. If there is no fresh pompano, don't expect to get frozen pompano from Australia—not even the waiters would serve that!! And where else would you find a mirliton made into a pirogue* stuffed with Louisiana crawfish? Blackened redfish was a local invention—our restaurateurs insist on improving standard dishes and creating new ones—all to prove that local creations continue to add to the art of the local kitchen.

Restaurants in New Orleans are located in every conceivable environment. They are housed in every conceivable type of structure: from

*A Cajun dugout canoe made of cypress.

the French Quarter to the Garden District, to both shores of Lake Pontchartrain, to both sides of the Mississippi, and to the posh suburban areas; in ante bellum mansions, in modern shopping centers and condos, in buildings in the Old French Market, in structures designed as restaurants, in warehouses, and even in a converted church. Truly, New Orleans is the Food Capital of the United States.

Phyllis Dennery

FOREWORD

Chef Paul Prudhomme's Cajun cuisine is music to the mouth—and Paul says that my jazz really cooks!

New Orleans' food and music are just two reasons the Crescent City has style and flavor all its own—and why there's only one New Orleans.

There are more than 2,500 restaurants in the Greater New Orleans area and Phyllis Dennery here introduces some of her favorites.

Paul, Phyllis, and I invite you to come to New Orleans and discover *your* favorite restaurant.

Dinner for Four

Angel Hair Pasta with Smoked Salmon

Zuppa Medici

Filetto di Manza Andrea

Rice Pilaf

Insalata Andrea

White Chocolate Mousse with Raspberry Sauce

Wines:

With the Appetizer—Pinot Grigio Santa Marguerita

With the Entrée—Gattinara Travaglini

Andrea Apuzzo and Roberto DeAngelis, Owners

Andrea Apuzzo, Chef

ANDREA'S

T here are several ways to train to become a noted chef. One can attend Cordon Bleu and La Varenne in France, the Culinary Institute of America, or, as Chef Andrea Apuzzo did, apprentice to the top chefs in Capri and then work through Switzerland, Germany, Mexico, Bermuda, and at last to his dream—opening his own restaurant in New Orleans.

By an unusual coincidence, he and his cousin, Roberto DeAngelis, met in the lobby of an Atlanta hotel which was trying to persuade Andrea to become its chef. The two men discovered their goal was the same, travelled to New Orleans, and, in driving around, located an available, handsome building in Metairie (a New Orleans suburb) and bought it on the spot.

Andrea and Roberto turned the building into an elegant, cozy, quiet restaurant with a great kitchen and excellent service. As in many fine restaurants, the chef obtains the best product and prepares it in the simplest way. There is no overpowering of seasonings nor combinations of food.

The presentation of the plate is the overriding concern. Hot must be served hot and cold must be cold. Guests such as Queen Elizabeth and Sophia Loren are among the famous who have enjoyed Andrea's talents over the years.

3100 Nineteenth Street
Metairie

ANGEL HAIR PASTA WITH SMOKED SALMON

6 ounces dry Capellini pasta
¼ cup butter
3 tablespoons chopped
   French dried shallots
1 tablespoon chopped garlic
4 ounces smoked salmon
¼ cup vodka

6 tablespoons white wine
1¼ cups whipping cream
   Salt and pepper
½ ounce domestic sturgeon
   caviar
   Parmesan cheese
   (optional)

1. Cook the pasta in boiling hot water with a touch of oil. Cook 3-4 minutes or until al dente. Drain the pasta and set aside.

2. In a skillet heat the butter; add the chopped shallots and garlic and sauté. Then add the salmon and mix well, until nicely blonde in color. Add the vodka and flame with a match. Let the vodka evaporate and add the white wine. Reduce one-third. Add the whipping cream. Let cook over a low flame for 10 minutes. Salt and pepper to taste.

3. Add the cooked pasta to the sauce and toss well.

4. Divide the pasta on four plates, topping each serving with ½ teaspoon sturgeon caviar.

Add Parmesan cheese if you wish.

ZUPPA MEDICI

1½ cups beef stock
1½ cups chicken stock
3 eggs

¼ cup Parmesan cheese
3 ounces cooked fresh
spinach

1. Start with a beef and chicken stock. In a soup pot add the broth together and bring to a boil. On an open fire in a metal bowl, add the eggs and Parmesan cheese along with the chopped spinach, and mix well with a whisk.

2. When the broth is boiling add the mixed ingredients to it and bring to a boil again. Take off the fire and serve immediately while hot.

Serve with hot Italian bread.

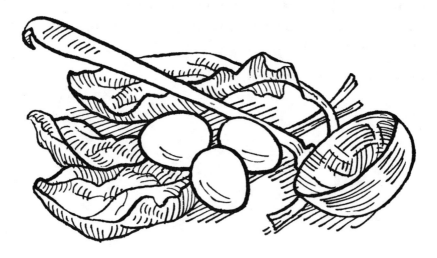

CAPRESE FILETTO DI MANZO

¼ cup vegetable oil
4 (7-ounce) beef fillets
½ cup butter
¼ cup fresh, sliced mushrooms
8 shrimp (21-25 count)
½ cup green and red bell
   peppers, cubed
1 tablespoon chopped shallots
1 medium clove garlic,
   minced

¼ cup brandy
6 tablespoons DEMI-GLACE
   SAUCE
½ cup whipping cream
1 teaspoon crushed black
   pepper
   Salt, to taste

1. In a skillet add the vegetable oil. When hot, add the fillets. Sauté to taste and remove the fillets.
2. Add to the skillet the butter, the sliced mushrooms, shrimp, green and red bell peppers, and sauté.
3. Add the chopped shallots and garlic and sauté until blonde in color.
4. Add the fillets again and flame with brandy.
5. Add the *DEMI-GLACE SAUCE* and whipping cream and simmer for 10 minutes. Add black crushed pepper and salt.

We suggest serving this entrée accompanied by seasonal fresh vegetables and rice pilaf.

DEMI-GLACE SAUCE

3 pounds veal bones
1 carrot, roughly chopped
1 onion, roughly chopped
3 celery sticks, roughly
   chopped
1 tablespoon tomato paste
¾ cup red wine
2 tablespoons flour

1 gallon water
¼ cup vegetable oil
2 bay leaves
½ teaspoon rosemary
½ teaspoon black
   peppercorns
Salt and pepper, to taste

1. Preheat the oven to 425°. In a roasting pan, roast the bones until light brown, about 25 minutes; add the vegetables and cook until they brown also, about 10 minutes more. Remove from oven.

2. Add the tomato paste, mix well, and add the red wine. Let the wine evaporate and sprinkle with flour, mixing well. Add the water and let come to a boil.

3. Add the herbs and salt and pepper to taste. Let simmer for 12 hours, stirring frequently.

4. Strain through a china cup (a form of cheesecloth) and bring to a boil again. Taste for seasoning. The sauce should have an even consistency and not be too thick. Reduce sauce by one-half.

RICE PILAF

½ cup chopped onions
2 tablespoons butter
1 cup uncooked rice
1½ cups chicken stock or
   bouillon

1 bay leaf
¼ teaspoon black pepper
Salt, to taste

1. Sauté the onions in the butter for 2 minutes.

2. In a baking pan mix together the sautéed onions, rice, chicken stock, bay leaf, pepper, and salt. Cover the pan. Bake at 375° for 30 minutes. Remove the pan from the oven, fluff the rice with a fork, and cook 10 minutes more, uncovered.

INSALATA ANDREA

8 pieces romaine with hearts
16 pieces Boston lettuce
8 ounces mushrooms, sliced
4 tomato wedges
8 slices avocado

Croutons
Green onion tips,
  chopped for garnish
1 cup ANDREA'S SALAD
  DRESSING

1. Tear all lettuce in half. Wash well, pat dry, and place on salad plates.

2. Arrange the rest of the ingredients on top and add *ANDREA'S SALAD DRESSING* and serve.

ANDREA'S SALAD DRESSING

1 egg
1 pinch black pepper
1 pinch white pepper
1 pinch dry mustard
½ teaspoon sugar
½ teaspoon salt
1 teaspoon minced garlic

1 teaspoon Dijon mustard
Juice of ½ lemon
¾ cup vegetable oil
1 teaspoon whipping cream
1 teaspoon white wine
  vinegar

1. Mix well the egg, seasonings, and Dijon mustard. Add the lemon juice.

2. Slowly add the vegetable oil while continuing to mix.

3. Stir in the whipping cream and white wine.

Andrea's salad dressing is delightful.

WHITE CHOCOLATE MOUSSE WITH RASPBERRY SAUCE

½ *pound melted white*
chocolate
3 *cups whipping cream*
2 *eggs, separated*

2 *tablespoons sugar*
1 *tablespoon hot water*
1 *tablespoon brandy*
Chocolate cups
RASPBERRY SAUCE

1. Melt the white chocolate. Whip the cream. In a separate bowl whip the egg whites to a light peak and add the sugar slowly.
2. In another bowl, mix the egg yolks, water, and brandy. Stir in the chocolate, egg whites, and make a liaison with the whipped cream and pipe into chocolate cups.
3. Let the mousse set in the refrigerator for at least 1 hour before serving.
4. Serve on a plate, setting the mousse in the center. Pass the *RASPBERRY SAUCE*.

RASPBERRY SAUCE

2 *pints raspberries*   ¼ *cup sugar*

Combine the raspberries with sugar and purée. Strain the sauce before serving.

This mousse will keep well in the refrigerator for one week.

Restaurant Antoine

Dinner for Six

Crawfish Cardinale

Chicken Rochambeau

Creamed Spinach

Brabant Potatoes

Baked Alaska

Cafe' Brulôt Diabolique

Wines:

Meursault

Montrachet

Bernard Guste, Proprietor

ANTOINE'S

In 1840, Antoine Alciatore opened Antoine's Restaurant. Today, 145 years later, it is a substantial house of culinary delights. Antoine's is the only restaurant in the United States owned and operated by the same family for over 145 years. Bernard "Randy" Guste, a fifth generation proprietor, holds the reins now, and Antoine's has never looked better nor had more spirit(s)!

Antoine's has received awards from Cartier, Holiday, Wine Spectators, and others. The 1985 San Francisco Chronicle's list of the best restaurants in the world places Antoine's eighth—and who could forget Frances Parkinson Keyes' famous novel, *Dinner at Antoine's?*

The establishment boasts fifteen fascinating dining rooms, including its newly reopened Japanese Room (which was closed from December 7, 1941, until this year) and the Rex Room. Rex is *the* King of New Orleans' Mardi Gras, and the room is decorated with photographs of former kings, antique invitations, and jewels worn by Mardi Gras royalty. The wine cellar is 168 feet long and contains 125,000 bottles. "My grandfather always said 'the best wine is the wine you like best'— and we are ready to please the taste of any guest," says Bernard.

The talent required to prepare proper soufflé potatoes has reached its peak at Antoine's. Its Filet Marchand de Vin and Filet Alciatore, as well as Oysters Ellis, Écrevisse (Crawfish) Cardinale, Escargot à la Bordelaise, and Oysters Foch are taste titillating delights to be found nowhere else in the world. The Pompano à la Pontchartrain (grilled pompano with sautéed crabmeat) is a pure delight.

The waiters at Antoine's, many there for over three decades, are part of the restaurant's charm. They are pleasant, helpful, and remember orders without benefit of pen and paper. And they can serve the meal without asking "Who's the Chicken Rochambeau"?

Randy says, "We are not just a family of restaurateurs, we're a breed." Antoine's is a gourmet shrine and a home of good cheer.

713 St. Louis Street

CRAWFISH CARDINALE

1 good bunch of green
    onions, chopped finely
10 tablespoons butter
½ cup dry white wine
1 soup spoon tomato paste
¼ teaspoon sugar
1 pound parcooked
    crawfish tails

Salt, to taste
White pepper, to taste
Tabasco sauce to taste
1½ cups CREAM SAUCE
Chopped parsley, for
    garnish
Buttered toast
    triangles, for garnish

1. Sauté the green onions in 6 tablespoons of butter until the onions lose their bright green color.
2. Add the white wine, tomato paste, and sugar and cook for about 5 minutes.
3. Add the crawfish, Tabasco, salt, and pepper and cook a few minutes until the crawfish are well seasoned.
4. Stir in 1½ cups of *CREAM SAUCE* until blended. Finish by stirring in 4 tablespoons of butter. Serve hot in ramekins garnished with chopped parsley and buttered toast triangles.

8 to 9 pounds of live boiled crawfish yield about 1 pound of picked meat.

Shrimp may be substituted for crawfish. Serve with toast points for lapping up the sauce.

CREAM SAUCE

1 *stick butter, melted*   1 *quart half and half*
1 *cup all-purpose flour*

1. Make a roux by melting the butter on a low heat and stirring in the flour until a yellow, smooth paste forms; set aside.
2. Heat the half and half until just before boiling, then wire whip the roux into the cream until thick. Remove from heat.

   This should make a thick cream sauce; a little will be left over after the craw-fish and spinach recipes are done. Cream sauce holds up in the refrigerator if necessary. Thinning can be achieved by adding additional cream in small amounts.

CHICKEN ROCHAMBEAU

6 *half chickens*   *ROCHAMBEAU SAUCE*
  Salt and pepper, to taste   *BÉARNAISE SAUCE*
6 *(1½-ounce) portions ham*

1. Bake the half chickens at 350° for 45 minutes. Remove the bones and hold warm in the oven.
2. For serving, have the chicken and ham hot in a oven. Place the portion of ham on the center of the plate; cover the ham and the bottom of the plate with *ROCHAMBEAU SAUCE*. Place chicken half on the ham and top with *BÉARNAISE SAUCE*. Garnish.

   Chicken Rochambeau is over 145 years old. The recipe, that is, not the chicken!

ROCHAMBEAU SAUCE

½ cup all-purpose flour
¾ cup melted butter
1 cup minced white onions
½ cup vinegar

½ cup sugar
2½ cups chicken stock
Salt and pepper, to taste
Caramel coloring

1. Blend the flour and ¼ cup melted butter to make a light roux; set aside. Sauté the onions with ½ cup of butter until limp, then add vinegar, sugar, and stock with salt and pepper and cook for 10 to 15 minutes.
2. Wire whip in the roux to get desired thickness and finish by coloring with caramel color. Run through a sieve if necessary.

BÉARNAISE SAUCE

1 soup spoon chopped
    tarragon in vinegar
    (drained of the vinegar)
2 soup spoons vermouth
½ cup minced white
    onions

9 egg yolks
    Cayenne pepper, to taste
2 tablespoons lemon juice
3 sticks butter, melted

1. Cook the tarragon, vermouth, and white onions until soft and blended; set aside.
2. Put into the blender the egg yolks, cayenne pepper, and lemon juice and blend by pulsing a few short times.
3. After the butter is melted, let it stand off the heat for 2 minutes. Then slowly add to the blender on medium speed. If needed, use a rubber spatula to work down all the sauce to blend thoroughly. Stir in the tarragon mixture.

ANTOINE'S

CREAMED SPINACH

3 (10-ounce) bags fresh
    spinach, washed and
    picked of large stems
Salt and pepper

2 cups CREAM SAUCE
    (see page 14)
1 stick lightly salted butter

1. In a covered pot, steam down the spinach in about ¾ cup of water and ½ teaspoon of salt. Drain in a collander then chop on a board or in a food processor.

2. Return the spinach to the pot and flavor with salt and pepper to taste, then blend in the 2 cups of CREAM SAUCE. Stir and, if necessary, run through a sieve. Finish by stirring in ½ to ¾ stick of butter.

Even children will enjoy this dish.

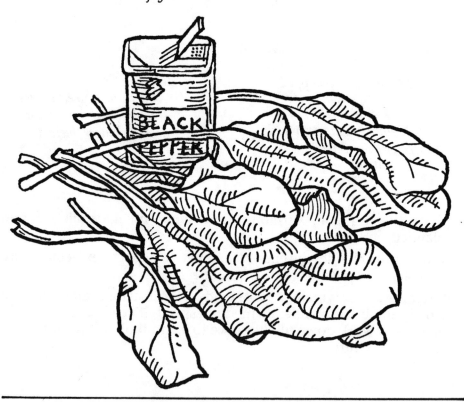

BRABANT POTATOES

6 *Idaho potatoes*   1½ *sticks butter*
   Salt

1. Use ¾-pound to 1-pound size potatoes for best results. Trim potatoes by cutting round ends off perpendicular to board, then across lengthwise on four sides to make a long box. Then cut to the shape and size of dice. There should be no skin on any piece.
2. In very lightly salted water, parboil the potatoes, being careful not to overcook. The potato needs to hold its shape during frying. Deep fry at 340° until golden brown.
3. For serving, melt the butter in a saucepan and turn the potatoes gently over a low heat. Sprinkle lightly with fine salt and serve hot.

Brabants were chosen over soufflé potatoes for this book because of the complicated process required to prepare the latter. When you visit Antoine's, ask your waiter to describe the technique.

ANTOINE'S

BAKED ALASKA

1 *pound cake*
8 *egg whites (large eggs)*

1½ *cups superfine sugar*
1 *quart vanilla ice cream*

1. Slice the pound cake in ½-inch thick slices; set aside. Beat the egg whites until foamy; add the sugar, a little bit at a time, until the egg whites hold a firm peak.

2. In an oven-proof platter, place a little meringue (whipped egg whites and sugar) on the center, then a layer of pound cake. Shape on the vanilla ice cream and mold to the shape of an oval dome.

3. Using hands, press the remaining pound cake (or an amount sufficient to cover the ice cream) around the ice cream. With a long, flat spatula, cover with the meringue and smooth to a dome shape.

4. With the oven on broil and the door open, hold the meringue close to broiler and turn, toasting the meringue. (Decorating with stiff meringue is optional.) Serve.

Oven mitts help greatly when holding the dessert under the broiler!

An elegant way to celebrate a festive occasion. Practice making doves and spelling names with stiff meringue to give the dessert a special touch.

CAFÉ BRULÔT DIABOLIQUE

2 sticks cinnamon	2 tablespoons sugar
8 cloves	6 tablespoons brandy
1 lemon peel	3 cups strong, hot coffee

Heat all ingredients in a bowl, except the coffee, which is heated in a pot. Stir the ingredients, pour in hot coffee, and serve. Add sugar to taste.

Antoine's method is to heat the ingredients in a heavy copper bowl and flame the bowl at the table. The flame is doused with the hot coffee and served into cups* designed especially for Café Brulôt at the restaurant.

*These cups may be found in New Orleans department stores and at special gift shops.

Dinner for Six

Crawfish O'Connor

Cream of Artichoke Soup

Veal Scallopini Gille

Watercress and Endive Salad with Cream Dressing

Strawberries Arnaud

Café Brulôt

Wines:

With the Appetizer and Soup—Chablis Premier Cru, Baron Patrick

With the Veal—Chateau Leoville Barton

Arshag Casbarian, Proprietor

Christian Gille, Chef

New Orleans is predominantly Catholic, but many revivalists visit the city and draw tremendous crowds. The Billy Graham of the restaurant business in this great old Creole community is Arshag (Archie) Casbarian—an Egyptian born Christian of Armenian descent—who took over the operation of the once great Arnaud's of the French Quarter and presided over its revival into one of the truly great restaurants of New Orleans.

Arnaud Cazenave opened his restaurant in 1918, and it rapidly became one of the three fine French restaurants in the city. Expanded from one building into a rabbit warren of eleven buildings—with more levels than Frank Lloyd Wright ever dreamed of—Arnaud's was the most popular businessman's luncheon establishment and meeting place in the city. Lavish dinner parties were held in the upper rooms, and one did not grow up in New Orleans without experiencing the thrill of a first meal of Shrimp Arnaud, Trout Meuniere, and Caramel Custard, accompanied by *the* most delicious cap bread imaginable.

Time took its toll, however, and after the passing of Arnaud, the proprietor became his daughter Germaine Cazenave Wells, who retained the façade and paid reverence to her parents.

Archie Casbarian, then the manager of the Royal Sonesta Hotel, across Bourbon Street from Arnaud's, was able to negotiate a lease of the restaurant with Mrs. Wells, and with his parents succeeded in bringing back to its former glory this wonderful tradition of New Orleans.

The food at Arnaud's remains, basically, the food served by its original owner, although new and lighter dishes now appear on the menu. Casbarian's philosophy is that the regular New Orleans customer knows what he wants to eat when he enters the restaurant. Archie does not care to make a "statement" of his own to his regulars, of whom there are many, but he and his chef Christian Gille have added to the menu for the benefit of his out-of-town guests.

In recognition of these achievements, Arnaud's has received the Travel/Holiday award for the past six years, the Cartier Four-Star Brass Plate, and the American Express award six times.

813 Bienville Street

CRAWFISH O'CONNOR

1 pound crawfish tails
6 tablespoons chopped
 shallots
3 tablespoons butter
3 tablespoons brandy

½ cup heavy cream
 AMORICAINE SAUCE
1 pinch cayenne pepper
 Salt and pepper, to taste

1. Sauté the crawfish and shallots in the butter over moderate heat. Add the brandy and flame.
2. Stir in the heavy cream. Add ¼ cup of the *AMORICAINE SAUCE*. Season to taste.

Serve in small ramekins.

AMORICAINE SAUCE

1 pound crawfish shells
2 tablespoons chopped
 shallots
1 bay leaf
1 tablespoon fresh chopped
 tomatoes
½ tablespoon peeled chopped
 carrots
1 tablespoon chopped white
 onions
2 tablespoons chopped celery

2 tablespoons butter
½ tablespoon tomato juice
1 tablespoon white wine
1 tablespoon brandy
1 cup water
1 cup heavy cream
 Salt and pepper, to taste
1 pinch paprika
1 pinch cayenne pepper

1. Clean the shells and break into coarse pieces.

2. Sauté the shallots, bay leaf, and vegetables in butter over high heat. Add the shells, tomato juice, white wine, and stir. Add the brandy and flame. Add the water and cream and blend. Season with salt, pepper, paprika, and cayenne. Simmer the sauce 30 minutes over moderate heat.

3. When the sauce is reduced to about one-half of its original quantity, strain and keep for reheating.

This is a French Creole classic, but in other parts of the country frozen crawfish may be substituted. We prefer fresh products whenever possible.

CREAM OF ARTICHOKE SOUP

1 stick (8 tablespoons) butter

6 fresh artichoke bottoms, uncooked and sliced

⅔ cup finely chopped white onions

1½ stalks celery, finely chopped

1 leek, cleaned and diced (white part only)

1 clove garlic, minced

1 large baking potato, peeled and diced

1 quart water

2¼ teaspoons salt

¼ teaspoon white pepper

1 cup (½ pint) whipping cream

2 tablespoons French brandy

1. Heat ¾ stick (6 tablespoons) of butter in a 3-quart saucepan. Sauté the artichoke bottoms, onions, celery, leek, and garlic for 7-10 minutes. Add the diced potato, the quart of water, salt, and pepper. Cover the pot, and simmer the soup for 20 minutes or until the potatoes become very soft. Add the whipping cream, the remaining ¼ stick (2 tablespoons) of butter, and the French brandy.

2. Ladle the contents of the pot into a blender and liquify. You will have to do this in several batches since there is more soup than will fit into the blender jar at one time. Pour the liquified contents into a bowl until all the soup has been blended.

3. Pour the bowl of soup back into the pot, rewarm, and serve.

ARNAUD'S

VEAL SCALLOPINI GILLE

2 tablespoons chopped
    shallots
¼ cup Marsala wine
1 pinch thyme
1 pinch basil
2 bay leaves
2 cups brown sauce
    Cornstarch
2 diced tomatoes

½ pound mushrooms,
    sliced
    Salt and pepper, to taste
6 (5-ounce) veal
    medallions
    Flour
½ cup butter
¼ bunch green onions,
    chopped

1. Reduce the shallots and Marsala wine to half quantity. Add the thyme, basil, and bay leaves and cook 10 minutes; then add the brown sauce. Reduce to half quantity. Add a little cornstarch (not too much) to make it thick. Add the diced tomatoes and mushrooms. Season with salt and pepper.

2. While the sauce is reducing, dip the veal in flour and sauté in butter for 2 minutes on each side. Place on a dinner plate, cover with the sauce, and decorate with chopped green onions in the center.

WATERCRESS AND ENDIVE SALAD

3 bunches watercress
3 endives
 Sliced mushrooms

12 cherry tomatoes
 CREAM DRESSING

1. Clean and wash the watercress and endives.
2. Place endive leaves around the outside of each plate with the watercress in the center. Sprinkle sliced mushrooms over the watercress and place 2 cherry tomatoes on each plate for decoration.
3. Cover with the CREAM DRESSING or serve separately.

CREAM DRESSING

½ cup mayonnaise
2 tablespoons sour cream
6 tablespoons Creole cream
 cheese
¼ bunch green onions,
 chopped

1 pinch green peppercorns
4 drops Tabasco
4 drops Worcestershire sauce
 Salt and white pepper,
 to taste

Whip the mayonnaise, sour cream, and Creole cream cheese until smooth. Add the rest of the ingredients. Blend thoroughly.

STRAWBERRIES ARNAUD

5 ounces fresh strawberries,
  plus 1 pint more
  for serving
WINE SAUCE

6 large scoops vanilla
  ice cream
Whipped cream
Toasted almond slices

1. Add 5 ounces of strawberries to the chilled WINE SAUCE. Let the strawberries marinate for at least 1 hour.

2. When ready to serve, in a large glass place 1 large scoop of vanilla ice cream. Cover with strawberries in WINE SAUCE and additional fresh strawberries. Top with whipped cream and toasted almond slices.

WINE SAUCE

2 cups Burgundy wine
¼ cup granulated sugar
3 cloves
1 pinch nutmeg

1 pinch cinnamon
Zest of ¼ orange
Zest of ¼ lime
3 drops vanilla

Boil all the sauce ingredients gently for about 15-20 minutes. Refrigerate for at least 1 hour.

This sauce may be made one day in advance.

CAFÉ BRULÔT

4 small cinnamon sticks,
   broken
3 dozen cloves
3 level teaspoons white sugar
2 lemons

French brandy (6 count,
   1001, 1002, etc.)—
   about 2 ounces
Grand Marnier (10-15
   count)—or to taste
1 orange
  Chicory coffee

1. Put the broken cinnamon sticks, 12-18 cloves, sugar, whole lemon rind, and six counts of the brandy and the Grand Marnier (add more Grand Marnier if you desire a sweeter taste) into a metal mixing bowl over a Sterno flame.

2. Start a peel of the orange at the navel to spiral to the bottom of the orange; do not detach the peel from the orange; add one clove to the peel every half inch. Pierce the orange at the navel with a fork. Set orange, orange peel, and fork aside.

3. Heat a ladle (using a ladle with a screen, if possible), then pour 1 shot of each liqueur into the heated ladle and ignite with the Sterno flame. With the bowl over the flame, hold the fork and orange over the bowl so that the peel spirals down into the bowl; from the top of the orange coil extending from the bottom of the orange, pour the burning liqueur very slowly into the top coil of the orange peel until the mixture in the bowl ignites. Continue pouring over the peel for several more ladles, then pour hot chicory coffee into the bowl.

4. When the flame in the bowl is extinguished, ladle the coffee into brulôt or demi-tasse cups and serve with a twist of lemon.

Pure coffee may be used, but the chicory coffee adds a special dimension.

Recipes for New Orleans flaming coffee vary at each restaurant.

Dinner for Six

Shrimp Rémoulade

Shrimp and Crab Okra Gumbo

Redfish Bon Ton

Bread Pudding and Whiskey Sauce

Wine:

Sauvignon Blanc

Dr. Wayne Pierce, Proprietor

Louise Joshua, Chief Cook

Ann McCollum and Tish Hicks, Assistants

When Houma dentist, Dr. Wayne Pierce, says, "Open wider, please," it's not because he wants to fill a cavity, but because he wants to carry on his family's tradition of filling his guests' mouths with some of the best Cajun food available in New Orleans.

Dr. Pierce's Uncle Alvin and Tante Alzina came from Bayou Lafourche with their country kitchen recipes and took over a popular bar and lunch restaurant in the warehouse district on Magazine Street in New Orleans. Soon the Bon Ton—by word of mouth (the Pierces have never advertised)—became one of the most popular luncheon establishments and, later, dinner restaurants in the city serving genuine Cajun food. Dr. Pierce says that "even if the recipes are followed, a good background in handling and preparing food helps to insure a greater quality of success."

The Bon Ton, now located in a remodeled 19th century building provides an ambiance that attracts people from everywhere. Dr. Pierce is a member of the Master Chefs Institute, and the restaurant has been recognized by the Mobil, Holiday, and other awards. The southern decor of wrought iron chandeliers, old fashioned ceiling fans, and brick walls, a room of bubbling people (some bubbling with the Pierce's famous Rum Ramsey, made from a secret family recipe) receiving superb service from a master kitchen, is a truly joyous place in which to dine.

The kitchen is in the charge of a happy lady, Louise Joshua, who has been on the scene for almost thirty-five years. Wayne Pierce says, "A good cook has an interest and understanding of food with some formal training and experience." Dr. Pierce and his wife Debbie oversee a full staff while greeting the guests.

The mixture of diners runs the gamut from the true New Orleans gourmet to the visitor from far lands who has heard of the Pierce's food, all of which proves that word of mouth is the best form of advertising. The Pierces' philosophy is to continue the delightful Cajun repasts of Alvin and Alzina.

401 Magazine Street

SHRIMP RÉMOULADE

24 (15-20 count) large
shrimp, with shells
4 lemon halves
2 onion halves
Salt and pepper
4 tablespoons Creole mustard
5 tablespoons Dijon
mustard

½ cup chopped green onions
1 teaspoon paprika
1 teaspoon sugar
½ cup olive oil
Shredded lettuce
Parsley, for garnish
Lemon slices, for garnish
Tomato wedges, for garnish

1. To prepare the shrimp, bring 1 quart of water to a boil. Add the lemon halves, onion halves, salt and pepper. Add the shrimp, with shells, to the boiling mixture. Boil 10 full minutes. Remove from the fire. Add several ice cubes to cool. Let the shrimp sit in the seasoned mixture for 15 minutes. Peel and devein the shrimp.

2. To prepare the rémoulade sauce, mix the Creole mustard and Dijon mustard, green onions, paprika, and sugar in a mixing bowl. Pour in the olive oil slowly while stirring constantly. Add ¼ cup water to dilute and to make a smooth consistency.

3. Place 4 shrimp per serving over a bed of shredded lettuce. Cover with rémoulade sauce. Garnish with parsley, sliced lemon, and a tomato wedge.

The unique preparation created by Alzina Pierce utilizes traditional seasoning, but it tastes different from any other rémoulade.

SHRIMP AND CRAB OKRA GUMBO

1 cup flour
1 cup vegetable oil
4 cups chopped okra
6½ quarts water
2 cups diced large onions
½ cup diced green bell peppers
½ cup chopped green onions (shallots)
½ cup diced celery

3 tablespoons chopped garlic
4 gumbo crabs, cleaned and cut in half
1 tablespoon tomato paste
2 pounds peeled shrimp (60-70 count)
Salt and pepper, to taste
⅓ cup chopped parsley
Steamed rice

1. Make a roux by mixing the flour in hot oil and stirring constantly using a thick frying pan. Stir until the roux is golden brown (use low-medium flame). Set aside.

2. Smother the okra in another pot in ½ quart of water until thick and mushy. Set aside.

3. Sauté the onions, bell pepper, green onions, celery, and garlic until limp in cooking oil in a gumbo pot. Add the roux to the seasoning and stir until well mixed. Add 6 quarts of water and bring to a boil. Add the smothered okra, crab, and tomato paste and allow to simmer 1 hour on medium flame, stirring occasionally to prevent burning.

4. Add the shrimp, salt, and pepper and simmer 1 more hour. The gumbo should be slightly thickened. Sprinkle the parsley over and serve on steamed rice.

Gumbo freezes well in airtight containers.

REDFISH BON TON

6 (8-ounce) redfish fillets	½ cup water
Salt, to taste	1 teaspoon flour
Black pepper, to taste	¾ pound lump crabmeat
Paprika, to taste	(approximately 2 cups)
3 sticks butter	½ cup white wine
Juice of 2 lemons	½ cup chopped parsley

1. Sprinkle both sides of the redfish fillets with salt, pepper, and paprika.
2. Melt 2 sticks of butter in a large skillet. Slightly brown the butter.
3. Place the seasoned redfish in the skillet, belly side down and cook for 2 minutes over medium heat. Add the lemon juice. Turn the fish over, add the water, then flour, and mix. Lightly sprinkle the fish again with paprika. Cover the fish and cook 8-10 minutes. Remove the cover and simmer for 2-3 minutes more until the fish is done.
4. Remove the fish from the skillet and place the fillets on heated plates.
5. Stir the sauce remaining in the skillet. If the butter separates, add a little more water and stir vigorously to achieve a sauce.
6. Place the crabmeat in another pan. Marinate it over low heat in 1 stick of butter and the white wine until hot. Serve the redfish topped with crabmeat and chopped parsley. Spoon some of the butter sauce over each serving.

Redfish is available in the Gulf region. If not in your market, trout may be substituted.

BREAD PUDDING AND WHISKEY SAUCE

BREAD PUDDING:
- 6 ounces stale French bread with crust
- 2 cups milk
- 2 eggs
- 1 cup sugar
- 1 stick margarine, softened
- 4 tablespoons vanilla
- ¼ cup raisins
- 1½ tablespoons butter or margarine, melted

WHISKEY SAUCE:
- ¾ cup sugar
- 1 egg
- 1 stick butter, melted
- ½-¾ cup Bourbon whiskey, or to taste

1. To make the PUDDING, break the bread in pieces and place it into a large bowl. Add the milk and let sit until the bread absorbs it. Add the eggs, sugar, margarine, vanilla, and raisins and mix well. Coat the bottom of the baking pan with the melted butter or margarine. Select a pan that will allow the pudding to rise 1½" in thickness (approximately 4"x6"x3" deep). Pour the bread mixture into the pan. Bake at 350° for approximately 45 minutes or until the pudding is firm and light golden brown. Let the pudding cool. Cut the pudding into individual portions; put each portion in a separate dessert dish.

2. To make the WHISKEY SAUCE, cream or mix the sugar and the egg. Add the melted butter and stir until the sugar is dissolved. A small amount of warm water (3 tablespoons) may be needed to aid in dissolving the sugar. Stir in the whiskey.

3. When ready to serve, pour the sauce over the pudding in individual dessert dishes and heat under the broiler.

Bread Pudding is teriffic to eat. I have never met anyone who didn't like it.

Breakfast for Eight

Eye Opener Absinthe Suissesse

Fresh Strawberries with Double Cream

Oyster and Crabmeat Soup

Eggs Hussarde

Bananas Foster

Wines:

Served through the Entrée—Pouilly Fuissé

Served with the Bananas Foster—Moët et Chandon Champagne

Owen E., Jr., Jimmy, and Ted Brennan, Proprietors

Michael Roussel, Chef

Breakfast at Brennan's is always a festive occasion—more eye openers, champagne, and wine are consumed than you can imagine.

Owen E. "Pip" Brennan, Jr. likes to say that "this experience is like it was 150 years ago, when people in beautiful surroundings were eating at tables overlooking flower-furbished patios. Because of the contrast between outside and in, one feels that there are two different restaurants—one by day and one by night. Sparkling candlelight lends itself to special events." When celebrities visit New Orleans, they often go to Brennan's for breakfast. Entertainers, world leaders, politicians, business figures, sports champions, and other noted personalities can be seen at Brennan's tables.

This restaurant was the dream of Owen E. Brennan along with some members of his family. In 1955 after operating a restaurant one block away, Owen found a handsome brick building, owned by Tulane University, which was for rent. Owen, a creative, responsible man, the oldest of seven brothers and sisters, conceived the idea of leasing the former Patio Royale and turning it into a beautiful restaurant and patio. It is tragic to report that Owen died just a short time after construction began. Owen's three sons ("Pip," Jimmy, and Ted) operate it to this day. The breakfast at Brennan's menu in this book was personally chosen by Owen, Jr.

Creole and French cuisine at Brennan's make "Pip," Jimmy, and Ted proud. "Pip" likes to say "the bouquet and the taste of Brennan's in New Orleans are the most unique in the United States."

417 Royal Street

ABSINTHE SUISSESSE

12 ounces absinthe
(Pernod, Ricard, etc.)
4 large egg whites
2 cups heavy cream

4 ounces Orgeat syrup
(simple syrup with a dash
of almond extract added)
2 cups crushed ice

Put all the ingredients into a blender and mix on high speed for 30 seconds. Serve in old fashion glasses.

A wonderful apéritif!

FRESH STRAWBERRIES WITH DOUBLE CREAM

2½ cups heavy cream
2 tablespoons sugar

1 teaspoon vanilla
6 cups fresh strawberries

Mix the heavy cream, sugar, and vanilla. Serve over fresh, cleaned strawberries, using about ¾ cup strawberries for each serving.

OYSTER AND CRABMEAT SOUP

1 cup butter
2 cups finely chopped celery
1 cup finely chopped green
  onions
1¼ cups flour
2 tablespoons finely
  chopped garlic
4 dozen large, freshly
  shucked oysters

12 cups oyster water (the oyster
   liquid plus sufficient water
   to make 12 cups)
4 bay leaves
1 teaspoon thyme
2 teaspoons salt
1 teaspoon white pepper
1 pound lump white
  crabmeat, picked over

1. Melt the butter over medium heat in a 6-quart heavy saucepan, then
   sauté the celery and green onions until tender but not browned, stirring frequently. Gradually stir in the flour and cook 5 minutes
   longer, stirring constantly, over low heat. Add all remaining ingredients, except the crabmeat, and simmer for 20 minutes. Remove
   the pan from the heat and scoop out the bay leaves with a slotted
   spoon or a long fork; discard.

2. After the soup is cooked and ready to serve, add in the lump crabmeat and stir gently to fold in. Then serve!

EGGS HUSSARDE

8 slices grilled Canadian bacon or ham	16 large eggs
8 slices grilled tomatoes	3 quarts water
8 slices Holland rusk or toast	2 cups white vinegar
	MARCHAND DE VIN SAUCE
	HOLLANDAISE SAUCE

1. Grill the ham and tomato slices and, if necessary, prepare the toast. Set aside to keep warm.

2. To poach the eggs, bring the water and vinegar to a boil in a large skillet or sauté pan. Keeping the water at a continuous low rolling boil, crack the eggs one by one into it. Cook until the egg whites are firm, about 2 minutes. Lift the poached eggs out of the water with a skimmer or slotted spoon, allowing the water to drain back into the pan. Place them on a heated platter while you assemble the dishes.

3. To assemble the dishes, first place a slice of toast on each warmed plate, then top with a slice of grilled ham. Ladle about ⅓ cup of *MARCHAND DE VIN SAUCE* over the ham. Carefully place 2 poached eggs side by side on the sauce, then top with about ½ cup *HOLLANDAISE SAUCE*. Garnish each portion with a slice of grilled tomato placed to one side and serve.

This is the most complex of the Brennan egg dishes, primarily because it has several elements which must be prepared separately. Since MARCHAND DE VIN SAUCE is relatively time-consuming to prepare, it is a good idea to make it in advance and enough for two different meals at one time. Simply keep it refrigerated in a sealed container.

MARCHAND DE VIN SAUCE

1¼ cups butter
1 tablespoon finely chopped garlic
1 cup finely chopped white onion
1 cup finely chopped green onion
1¼ cups finely chopped parsley
1 cup finely chopped mushrooms
1 cup finely chopped boiled ham
1 cup flour

1 teaspoon salt
1 teaspoon black pepper
1 tablespoon thyme
3 bay leaves
½ cup Worcestershire sauce
1 quart beef stock
1 cup dry red wine

To prepare the *MARCHAND DE VIN SAUCE*, melt the butter in a heavy saucepan over low heat. Add the chopped vegetables and ham and cook until the vegetables are slightly soft. Sprinkle in the flour, salt, and pepper and stir to mix. Cook for about 4 minutes, then add the Worcestershire, beef stock, wine, thyme and bay leaves. Mix thoroughly and simmer over low heat, stirring very frequently, until the sauce is very thick and a rich brown color, about 1 hour. Place the pan of sauce in a warm oven or over the pilot on the surface of the stove to keep it warm while you prepare the other ingredients. Remove the bay leaves before serving.

HOLLANDAISE SAUCE

8 large egg yolks
4 tablespoons lemon juice
1½ pounds hot melted butter, clarified

1 teaspoon salt
¼ teaspoon cayenne pepper, approximately

To prepare the *HOLLANDAISE SAUCE*, put the egg yolks and lemon juice in a mixing bowl. Place the bowl over or near the pilot on top of the stove. Beat briefly with a whisk, then slowly pour in the hot melted butter, beating briskly and constantly while you pour. When the sauce begins to thicken, sprinkle in the salt and pepper. Continue to beat while adding the rest of the butter. Beat until the sauce reaches an attractive, thick consistency. When the sauce is finished, leave the bowl over the pilot to keep warm, or place it in a basin of warm water.

BANANAS FOSTER

8 tablespoons butter	8 bananas, cut in half
2 cups brown sugar	lengthwise, then halved
1 teaspoon cinnamon	½ cup rum, approximately
8 teaspoons banana liqueur	8 scoops vanilla ice cream

1. Melt the butter over an alcohol burner in a flambé pan or attractive skillet. Add the sugar, cinnamon, and banana liqueur and stir to mix. Heat for a few minutes, then place the halved bananas in the sauce and sauté until soft and slightly browned. Add the rum and allow it to heat well, then tip the pan so that the flame from the burner causes the sauce to light. Allow the sauce to flame until it dies out, tipping the pan with a circular motion to prolong the flaming.

2. Place the scoops of ice cream in serving dishes. Lift the bananas carefully out of the pan and place 4 pieces over each portion of ice cream, then spoon the hot sauce from the pan over the top.

This can also be prepared over a stove burner, then brought to the table and flamed.

CAFE SBISA

Dinner for Four

Oysters en Brochette

Mixed Fried Vegetables

Hickory Grilled Lamb Chops with Stuffed Tomatoes

Red New Potatoes with Sour Cream

Spinach Salad with Creole Mustard Vinaigrette

Chocolate Sin Cake

Wines:

With the Oysters—Muscadet, Barre

With the Lamb—Cabernet Sauvignon, Beaulieu

Dr. Larry Hill and John Pico, Owners

Anthony Monroe, Chef

One would hardly think that a child psychiatrist, an antique shop owner, and a patron of the arts would use *his* spare time to develop a restaurant in the Vieux Carré in New Orleans. But Dr. Larry Hill has done just that.

Larry and John Pico, another wine and food gourmet, found a building constructed before 1818 across from the French Market and operated by the Sbisa family as a coffee house, oyster bar, and café since 1899, and with the help of a talented young architect have restored the old ship chandlery into a restaurant which emphasizes simplicity—but don't let that word mislead you.

Dr. Hill and Mr. Pico have raised the cooking of American and foreign foods to the epitome of Creole perfection, and have treated food indigenous to the region in a similar manner. There is no better half-shell bar in the area, and the proprietors post a "fine wine by the glass" list—changed every day—which permits guests to select a wine for each course. Café Sbisa offers the finest in Scotch salmon, oysters, and clams at the half shell bar and at the table, and the kitchen develops Creole Bay Scallops, Cajun fresh salmon pâté, and hickory grilled lamb among many other delicious dishes.

This is a neighborhood restaurant, patronized by local and nationally known artists, politicians, fellow restaurateurs, patrons of the arts, and visitors to New Orleans. A balanced noise level is created by a pianist on the balcony and sufficient space between tables to permit conversation. The waiters are willing and able to make suggestions if requested, but are not overbearing in their manner.

Anthony Monroe, a young New Orleans trained chef, presides over the kitchen and carries out the proprietors' aims to perfection. Hill and Pico take pride in operating a warm, friendly, cheerful, and, nevertheless, very sophisticated restaurant, serving the best foods treated in a simple yet worldly manner. As Dr. Hill expresses it: "We have substance without excess."

Café Sbisa is a "late" restaurant, and its guests are happy people. The restaurant has received awards from *Egon Ronay, The In Guide,* and *Who's Who in American Restaurants,* as well as from numerous local critics.

1011 Decatur Street

OYSTERS EN BROCHETTE

8 slices bacon	1 stick unsalted butter
24 plump Louisiana oysters	4 slices toasted
Egg wash	French bread
1 cup yellow corn flour*,	Chopped parsley,
seasoned with salt, pepper,	for garnish
and cayenne pepper	4 lemon wedges, for garnish
Vegetable oil, for frying	

1. Cut the bacon strips into thirds and parboil for 2-3 minutes. Dry on paper towels. Thread alternating strips of bacon with oysters on a 6-inch skewer. Dip into egg wash. Roll in seasoned corn flour. Fry in vegetable oil to cover until light brown and the bacon is crisp. Drain on paper towels.

2. Brown the butter in a small skillet. Remove the oysters and bacon from the skewer; place on the slices of toasted French bread. Pour browned butter over the oysters. Garnish each serving with chopped parsley and a large lemon wedge.

OYSTERS EN BROCHETTE may be served as an entrée.

Available in some gourmet or specialty shops.

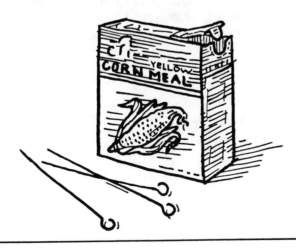

MIXED FRIED VEGETABLES

1 *small eggplant, peeled and pared into strips of ¼"x¼"x3"*

½ *pound fresh button mushrooms, brushed, with stems pared*

¼ *cup sliced hamburger dills, dried between paper towels*

½ *bunch curly parsley, with stems trimmed*

EGG WASH

French breadcrumbs

Salt and pepper

Fresh thyme

Vegetable oil, for frying

1. Dip the prepared vegetables in the *EGG WASH*.
2. Dredge in fresh French breadcrumbs lightly seasoned with salt, pepper, and fresh thyme.
3. Fry in hot vegetable oil deep enough to cover until light brown.
4. Drain on paper towels. Place in a napkin-lined basket and serve immediately.

An excellent hot hors d'oeuvre with cocktails. At Café Sbisa we would recommend a Sazerac.

Sazerac for one: In one glass swirl Herbsaint until coated. In another glass place a dash of Peychaud's and Angostura bitters, 1 ounce of rye whiskey, simple syrup to taste, and fill with ice and strain into the first glass. Add two cubes of ice and a twist of lemon.

EGG WASH

¼ *cup yellow corn flour*
¼ *cup unbleached flour*
1 *pint milk*

1 *egg*
Salt and cayenne pepper, to taste

Combine all ingredients.

HICKORY GRILLED LAMB CHOPS WITH STUFFED TOMATOES

12 tender trimmed lamb chops,
    loin or rib according
    to preference
1 cup olive oil
2 sprigs fresh rosemary or
    1 teaspoon dried rosemary

Juice of 1 lemon
STUFFED TOMATOES
Watercress, for garnish

1. Place the lamb chops into a marinade made up of olive oil, rosemary, and lemon juice. Marinate for at least 2 hours, but preferably overnight.
2. When ready to serve, place the chops on a grill over medium-hot coals of hickory wood or charcoal. Grill until the desired degree of doneness is reached, turning once.
3. Place a stuffed tomato in the center of each plate, surround with three lamb chops, and garnish with a sprig of fresh watercress.

Coals of mesquite may be used for this recipe, but we prefer the hickory flavor.

STUFFED TOMATOES

4 large vine-ripened
    tomatoes
1 cup breadcrumbs
¼ cup fresh chopped parsley
2 teaspoons fresh basil

2 teaspoons fresh chopped
    thyme
¼ cup plus 2 tablespoons
    olive oil
Salt and pepper, to taste

1. Slice off the top of each tomato. Hollow out, saving the pulp.
2. Mix the chopped pulp with the rest of the ingredients, using ¼ cup of olive oil. Fill the tomatoes with the mixture. Dribble the tops with the remaining olive oil.
3. Place in hot oven (450°) for 10 minutes, or until brown but still firm.

RED NEW POTATOES WITH SOUR CREAM

20 *small red new potatoes*   1 *cup sour cream*
    Salt

1. Scrub, but do not peel, the new potatoes.
2. Boil in salted water 10 minutes or until tender when pierced.
3. Serve in a large bowl with accompanying bowl of sour cream.

SPINACH SALAD WITH CREOLE MUSTARD VINAIGRETTE

½ *cup olive oil*   *Salt and pepper, to taste*
3 *tablespoons red wine vinegar*   1 *pound fresh spinach, washed*
1 *tablespoon Creole mustard*   *and trimmed of large stems*
   (any whole grain brown
   mustard will substitute)

1. Mix the olive oil, vinegar, Creole mustard, salt and pepper.
2. Toss with chilled spinach leaves.

This salad can be garnished with crumbled fried bacon and thinly sliced fresh mushrooms if desired.

CHOCOLATE SIN CAKE

10 ounces unsalted butter at
  room temperature, plus
  butter for the pan
10 ounces semi-sweet
  chocolate

1½ cups sugar
8 large eggs
  COFFEE WHIPPED CREAM

1. Liberally butter a 9"x1½" round cake pan. Line the bottom with wax paper and butter the paper. Preheat the oven to 350°.
2. In the top of a double boiler, melt the chocolate over hot water. Add the butter and stir until the butter has melted and the mixture is smooth.
3. Remove from the heat. Whisk the sugar gradually into the chocolate mixture until the mixture is thick. In a separate bowl, beat the eggs until they are foamy. Then stir them into the chocolate mixture until they are well incorporated.
4. Pour the mixture into the prepared pan and place the pan in a 14"x 11" baking pan. Add enough boiling water to come halfway up the side of the baking pan. Bake in the center of the oven for 1½ hours.
5. Remove the cake pan and let set for 10 minutes. Invert onto a plate. Serve at room temperature with *COFFEE WHIPPED CREAM*.

COFFEE WHIPPED CREAM

1 cup heavy cream
2 tablespoons powdered sugar

1 tablespoon strong coffee

1. Beat the heavy cream until it just begins to hold shape.
2. Sift the powdered sugar over the top and beat until the cream holds soft peaks.
3. Stir in the strong coffee. Spoon onto the cake for each serving.

Christian's Restaurant

Dinner for Four

Oysters Roland

Salmon au Poivre Vert

French Fried Eggplant

Pecan Torte

Wine:

Robert Stemmler Chardonnay

Christian Ansel, Proprietor

Roland Huet, Chef

CHRISTIAN'S

Have you ever gone to church for a gourmet meal? Of course, if you've gone to Christian's, now located in a beautifully converted Lutheran church, originally constructed in 1904, which has won national recognition for its architecture as well as for its cuisine.

In 1973 Chris Ansel and his wife moved from his family's famous restaurant, Galatoire's, and opened their first restaurant in a suburb of New Orleans. Their immediate success prompted them to move nearer to the center of town—to an old established neighborhood—where they were able to purchase the church they now occupy.

The restaurateurs charged their architect to retain the character of the church while converting the building. Guests now are greeted in the vestibule, and, if the table is not ready, they await their turn in a comfortable pew, or they may step up to a tiny bar in what once was the "crying room for tots in the flock." If one wishes to powder her nose, she will find the correct location is behind the altar. The ceiling with its original beams and the windows with their original amber lights add to the authenticity of the restoration.

Easily accessible from all parts of the city, and with a large parking space available, Christian's is an extremely popular rendezvous for local and visiting gourmets. Congenial service and great food are available at lunch and dinner.

3835 Iberville Street

OYSTERS ROLAND

½ bunch parsley
1 clove garlic
1 (6-ounce) can mushrooms,
   stems and pieces, with
   juice reserved
½ pound butter, softened

½ teaspoon black pepper
½ teaspoon salt
⅛ teaspoon nutmeg
½ cup breadcrumbs
2 dozen oysters, poached
   until they curl

1. Blend in a high-speed food processor, such as Cuisinart, in this order: parsley, garlic, and mushrooms. Blend well until the parsley is finely chopped; then add the butter and spices and blend again. Now add mushroom juice and breadcrumbs and blend well.

2. Place 6 poached oysters each in 4½-inch au gratin dishes, smooth the butter mixture over, and put under the broiler until brown and bubbly.

If a food processor is not available, a meat grinder may be substituted using the smallest plate for grinding parsley, garlic, and mushrooms and blending after with a mixer.

This recipe is as charming as the chef.

SALMON AU POIVRE VERT

4 (10-ounce) salmon fillets
   (or any other firm fish)
2 teaspoons green
   peppercorns

1 cup white wine
1 pint whipping cream
   Pinch of salt

1. Poach the fillets in fish stock or sauté them in a buttered pan. Drain the fillets and keep warm.
2. Put the green peppercorns in a sauté pan and add the wine. Cook until the wine is almost dry and add the cream. Reduce the cream until thick and season with salt and more green peppercorns if desired.
3. Spoon the sauce over the fillet of fish and serve immediately.

For a beautiful presentation, garnish with lemon slices, capers, and curly parsley.

FRENCH FRIED EGGPLANT

2 eggplants
  Flour
  EGG WASH*

Breadcrumbs
Peanut oil, for frying

1. Peel and cut two eggplants into long ½-inch strips. Dredge the strips in flour, pass them into an *EGG WASH**, and shake them in bread-crumbs.
2. Heat a deep fryer with peanut oil to 375°. Cook the strips until golden brown, turning them frequently.

This can be served as a vegetable seasoned with salt and pepper or as an hors d'oeuvre seasoned with powdered sugar.

**To make an EGG WASH, simply beat 1 whole egg.*

CHRISTIAN'S

PECAN TORTE

1 cup brown sugar, sifted
1 cup powdered sugar, sifted
2 eggs
1 cup butter, softened
½ teaspoon vanilla

1 cup chopped pecans
8 ounces coconut macaroons, crumbled
Vanilla ice cream
Chocolate sauce (optional)

1. Mix well all ingredients except the ice cream and chocolate sauce with a wooden spoon in a bowl and refrigerate. When firm, roll in heavy aluminum foil to desired diameter and freeze.

2. When ready to serve, unwrap, and slice the roll. Place a scoop of vanilla ice cream on top of each slice. Serve immediately. If desired, put hot chocolate sauce on top.

To decorate the plate, add maraschino cherries and leaves—mint, if available.

Commander's Palace

Dinner for Four

Oysters Trufant

Crabmeat and Corn Bisque

Veal with Wild Mushrooms

Creole Succotash Timbale

Commander's Salad and Dressing

Blueberry Shortcake

Café Noir

Wines:

With the Appetizer—Robert Mondavi Chardonnay, 1982

To Follow—Jordan Alexander Valley Cabernet Sauvignon, 1980

Ella, Dick, John and Dottie Brennan, Proprietors

Emeril Lagasse, Chef

COMMANDER'S PALACE

Ella, Dick, John, and Dottie Brennan work together to present a restaurant where the ambiance is the finest and the cuisine is unmatched.

The mere words "Creole cuisine" tend to stimulate appetites. Taste buds tingle at the very thought of salty oysters from the Barataria marshes, blue-claw crabs from Lake Pontchartrain, crawfish from the Atchafalaya swamps, rich gumbos thickened with pulverized leaves from sassafras trees, and those prickly green vegetables from the mirliton vines. With such exotic ingredients, Creole cooks, over the years, have created dishes that are world-renowned.

Commander's new Haute Creole cuisine takes those same luscious ingredients, even some of the same basic recipes, a step further in the continuing evolution of this unique cuisine. The results are dishes that are lighter, more subtle, yet every bit as delicious.

Fish, for example, are grilled quickly, removed from the fire while the meat is still flaky and moist. Oysters are poached only until their sides curl. Meats are instantly seared so that they retain their natural flavors and juices. Vegetables are served crisp and crunchy. Sauces are made from rich stocks that have been simmering for hours, reduced by evaporation to the purest essences of taste and aroma.

The new Haute Creole cuisine retains the richness and excellence for which this regional cuisine is famed. At the same time, a new purity, simplicity, and elegance create dishes that are lighter, fresher in texture and body.

Ella Brennan, recently named National Restaurateur of the Year, and her sisters and brothers have developed Commander's Palace, located in a beautiful 19th century mansion in the heart of the historic Garden District, into one of the outstanding restaurants in this city of cuisine.

1403 Washington Avenue

OYSTERS TRUFANT

¾ quart heavy cream
3 dozen freshly shucked
    oysters
    (reserve all liquor)

1 teaspoon CREOLE
    SEAFOOD SEASONING
Caviar, for garnish
Green onions, for garnish

1. Place the cream and all of oyster liquor from the oysters in a sauce-pan gently simmering until reduced to 1½ cups.
2. When reduced, add 1 dozen of the oysters and cook for 5 minutes. Strain out the oysters, and discard, leaving the sauce.
3. Take the remaining 2 dozen oysters and place them in a hot skillet with *CREOLE SEAFOOD SEASONING (no oil!)* and toss gently to warm the oysters. Do not overcook! When oysters are warmed, drain on a towel, place on a serving dish, and cover with sauce. Garnish with caviar or chopped green onions.

For this recipe, you may use domestic caviar, which is found in most grocery stores.

CREOLE SEAFOOD SEASONING

2 tablespoons dried
    oregano
⅓ cup salt
¼ cup granulated garlic
¼ cup black pepper
2 tablespoons cayenne
    pepper

2 tablespoons dried
    thyme
⅓ cup paprika
3 tablespoons granulated
    onion

Combine all ingredients and mix thoroughly. Pour into a large glass jar and seal airtight. Keeps indefinitely.

Makes 2 cups.

If black pepper is not to your taste, reduce the quantity to one half.

CRABMEAT AND CORN BISQUE

½ cup butter
½ cup all-purpose flour
1 quart CRAB STOCK
   Kernels from 2 ears
    sweet corn

¾ cup heavy cream
½ pound lump crabmeat,
   picked over
   Salt and pepper, to taste
¾ cup finely chopped
   green onions

1. In a 5-quart saucepan melt the butter. Add the flour and cook, stirring, until the flour begins to stick to the pan. Add the *CRAB STOCK*. Bring to a boil, stirring constantly, then simmer 15 minutes. Add the corn and simmer for 15 minutes more. Pour in the cream and stir well. Gently add the crabmeat.

2. Remove from the heat and let stand for 15 minutes for the flavors to blend.

3. Reheat gently to serving temperature so that the lump crabmeat does not break into flakes. Add salt and pepper to taste. Just before serving add the green onions.

To hold for serving or to reheat, use a double boiler.

CRAB STOCK

5 medium-size hard-shell
  crabs

2 quarts water
2 medium onions, quartered

Combine all ingredients and cook for 45 minutes.

VEAL WITH WILD MUSHROOMS

8 veal cutlets, about 3 ounces each, well pounded
CREOLE MEAT SEASONING
3 tablespoons unsalted butter
4 medium shallots, chopped
4 ounces fresh, wild mushrooms (chanterelles or morels)
2 ounces cultivated mushrooms

2 tablespoons brandy
¼ cup red wine
¾ cup demi-glace
¼ cup heavy cream
Salt and freshly ground black pepper
Watercress or parsley, for garnish

1. Season the veal with *CREOLE MEAT SEASONING* and sauté in hot melted butter until lightly browned on both sides, turning once. Remove and keep warm.

2. To the butter remaining in the pan, add the shallots and mushrooms and sauté for 1 minute. Add the brandy, wine, demi-glace, and cream. Add salt and pepper if needed, and simmer for about 5 minutes.

3. To serve, arrange the veal on a warm serving plate, ladle sauce over the veal, and garnish with watercress or parsley.

Morels and chanterelles, wild mushrooms usually imported from Switzerland or France, are available either fresh or dried in specialty food shops or at Oriental greengrocers.

CREOLE MEAT SEASONING

1 cup salt
¾ cup granulated or
    powdered garlic
¾ cup freshly ground
    black pepper

½ teaspoon cayenne pepper,
    or to taste
¼ cup paprika

Combine all ingredients and mix thoroughly; pour into a large glass jar; seal tightly. Keeps indefinitely.

Makes 3 cups.

CREOLE SUCCOTASH TIMBALE

½ medium onion, chopped
2 cloves garlic
1 ear fresh corn
    (kernels removed)
½ tablespoon butter
¼ pound okra
2-3 ounces andouille sausage,
    diced
½ cup canned diced tomatoes

¼ cup blanched fresh
    lima beans
¼ cup rich chicken stock
1 tablespoon Worcestershire
    sauce
½ teaspoon hot sauce
½ cup diced green onion
3 eggs

1. Lightly sauté the onion, garlic, and corn in butter. Add the okra and andouille and simmer 10 minutes. Add all remaining ingredients except the eggs and simmer an additional 5 minutes.
2. Let the mixture cool, then mix in 3 whole eggs. Fill buttered timbales. Bake at 300° until firm, approximately 45 minutes.

Andouille enhances the flavor. If not available, a good polish sausage will come close.

COMMANDER'S SALAD

4 cups mixed fresh
   salad greens
4 tablespoons crisply cooked,
   crumbled bacon

4 tablespoons freshly grated
   Parmesan cheese
COMMANDER'S DRESSING
2 hard-cooked eggs, halved

1. Wash, dry, and tear the salad greens into bite-size pieces. Combine in a mixing bowl with the bacon and cheese.

2. To serve, pour the *COMMANDER'S DRESSING* over the mixture in a salad bowl and toss. Divide onto individual salad plates or bowls and garnish each serving with half an egg.

COMMANDER'S DRESSING

1½ cups salad oil
1 egg, at room temperature
⅓ teaspoon salt

½ teaspoon freshly cracked
   black pepper
¼ cup vinegar
3 tablespoons minced onion

Put ½ cup oil and the egg in a blender with remaining ingredients. Cover and blend on low speed. Remove cover and gradually pour in the remaining oil. Mix thoroughly using a whisk.

BLUEBERRY SHORTCAKE

SHORTCAKE:
>   2 *cups flour*
>   ½ *cup sugar*
>   ¾ *tablespoon baking powder*
>   ½ *teaspoon salt*
>   ½ *cup shortening*
>   6 *tablespoons milk*
>   2 *eggs*
>   *Butter*

BLUEBERRY SAUCE:
>   ¼ *cup sugar*
>   ¼ *cup Grand Marnier*
>   ¼ *cup water*
>   2 *pints blueberries*
>
> *Whipped cream, for garnish*

1. Sift together the flour, sugar, baking powder, and salt. Cream the shortening with the dry ingredients. Add the milk and eggs and incorporate until smooth. Let the dough sit at room temperature for at least ½ hour.

2. Roll the dough on a floured surface to ½-inch thickness. Cut with a biscuit or cookie cutter. Bake at 375° on parchment paper for 14-16 minutes until golden brown. When removing from the oven, brush with butter. Cool.

3. To make the Blueberry Sauce, mix the sugar, Grand Marnier, and water. Add the blueberries and let sit for ½ hour. Serve over shortcakes with fresh whipped cream.

COMMANDER'S PALACE

CAFÉ NOIR

A good Creole cook never boils coffee, but drips it slowly until all the flavor is extracted. (The modern Chemex and other drip coffeemakers using paper filters work very well.) Allow 1 rounded tablespoon coffee per cup, pour in freshly boiled water (overboiled water spoils the flavor), wait for the rich, fragrant aroma to arise, and serve in fine china cups.

A lemon zest adds a different twist.

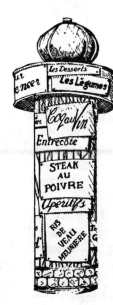

Crozier's

Dinner for Six

Fish Mousse Nantua

Asparagus Mousseline

Tournedos Perigueux

Artichokes Florentine

Salade Mimosa

Floating Island

Wines:

Mersault

Pommard

Gerard and Eveline Crozier, Proprietors

Gerard Crozier, Chef

CROZIER'S

Chef Gerard Crozier and his wife, Eveline, in 1976, offered their talents as restaurateurs to residents and visitors alike. They opened their restaurant in the eastern end of New Orleans, a new residential section of the city, but in a very short time residents of the older sections of the city found their way to the charming and cozy restaurant decorated in the French Provincial style.

Crozier's is a true French restaurant and is the only New Orleans establishment honored by *Bon Appétit* as "Best of the Best." The ambiance, the service, and the cuisine continue to be excellent.

Chef-owner Gerard Crozier apprenticed in several fine restaurants in France and Switzerland, notably Oustau de Beaumaniere in Les Baux. Gerard cooks much of the food himself to keep a high quality. His cooking is mostly French regional cuisine.

Crozier's is the type of restaurant worth seeking, even if one lives on the western end of the city. One can reach it easily on Highway I-10 East, leaving the Interstate at the Read Road exit, then turning left on Read Road to the service road known as Read Lane, where you will find ambrosia under the nom de plume "Crozier's."

7033 Read Lane

FISH MOUSSE NANTUA

1½ pounds firm fish
    (¾ pound trout and
    ¾ pound salmon or
    1½ pounds of either one)
10 tablespoons butter

5 eggs
1 cup heavy cream
½ cup PANADE
    SAUCE NANTUA
6 whole shrimp, for garnish

1. Put the fish through a grinder or food processor.
2. Add the butter and eggs, one at a time, and beat in the cream by hand. Mix well with the *PANADE*.
3. Grease six individual ramekins and fill to the top with mousse. Place in a baking pan half filled with water. Bake for 40 minutes at 350°.
4. Remove from the oven, turn ramekins upside down, and empty on a platter. Cover with *SAUCE NANTUA*. Put one whole shrimp on each mold for decoration.

PANADE

1 cup milk
2 tablespoons butter

¼ cup flour
Salt and pepper, to taste

Heat the milk and butter in a saucepan. When boiling, turn to very low heat and whisk in the flour and seasoning until thick. Set aside.

SAUCE NANTUA

2 tablespoons SHRIMP
  BUTTER
2 tablespoons flour
1½ cups milk

½ cup chopped shrimp
  (reserve heads and shells)
½ cup sautéed mushrooms
  (canned caps may be
  substituted)

In a saucepan melt the *SHRIMP BUTTER*. Slowly add the flour and whisk until foamy. Do not brown. Add the milk, ½ cup at a time. Cook until the sauce thickens; add the shrimp and mushrooms. Cover with plastic wrap to prevent film from forming if you are not using the sauce immediately.

SHRIMP BUTTER

Shrimp heads and tails
  (reserved from SAUCE
  NANTUA)
Salt, thyme, and white
  pepper

2 cups water
1 stick butter

Slowly boil the reserved shrimp heads and shells with seasoning in the water and stick of butter for 15 minutes. Strain into a saucepan and refrigerate. When the butter rises to the top and hardens, remove and wrap well in plastic wrap. Shrimp butter will freeze well.

ASPARAGUS MOUSSELINE

72 *spears of baby asparagus*   *SAUCE MOUSSELINE*

Peel the asparagus and boil in salted water until tender. Do not over-cook. Drain and set aside. Serve 12 asparagus to each person, top-ped with *SAUCE MOUSSELINE.*

SAUCE MOUSSELINE

3 *egg yolks*
12 *tablespoons butter, melted*
Juice of ½ lemon

Salt and pepper, to taste
6 *tablespoons heavy cream*

1. Whip the egg yolks with a little water on the stove in a bain marie until hot and double the volume. Add the melted butter, lemon juice, salt, and pepper.
2. Whip the heavy cream, and add to the sauce. Serve on the side of the asparagus.

This SAUCE MOUSSELINE is a delicious version of the popular hollan-daise sauce.

TOURNEDOS PERIGUEUX

12 (3-ounce) tournedos
   Salt and pepper, to taste
   Oil and butter, for
    sautéing
12 slices goose liver pâté

2 pounds mushrooms
   SAUCE PERIGUEUX
   Chopped parsley, for
    garnish

1. Season the meat with salt and pepper. Sauté until rare or done to choice in hot oil and butter. Place on serving platter with a slice of pâté on each piece of meat.

2. Sauté the mushrooms. Arrange around the meat. Pour SAUCE PERIGUEUX over the meat. Sprinkle chopped parsley over the top.

SAUCE PERIGUEUX

½ pound lean ground beef
½ onion, chopped
1 small carrot, chopped
¼ cup cooking brandy
1 quart red wine
1 teaspoon tomato paste

   Thyme
1 bay leaf
   Roux
1 truffle
2 tablespoons goose liver
   pâté

1. Sauté in very hot oil the meat, onions, and carrots. Pour the brandy over and reduce; add the wine, tomato paste, thyme, and bay leaf. Cook for 45 minutes very slowly.

2. Thicken the sauce with a little bit of roux (flour and butter). Strain, then add the chopped truffle and goose liver pâté. Mix and serve over the tournedos.

The chef likes to use a red Burgundy, but any dry red wine may be substituted.

The sauce is such a wonderful color, no garnish is necessary for this handsome presentation.

ARTICHOKES FLORENTINE

6 *artichokes*   1 *pound fresh spinach*
   Unsalted butter

1. Boil the artichokes in salted water until tender. Remove and cool.
2. When cold, remove the leaves and chokes from the bottoms.
3. Heat the bottoms in unsalted butter.
4. Sauté the fresh spinach. Put the spinach in the artichoke bottoms and serve very hot.

A minced clove of garlic adds flavor to the spinach. Bread crumbs sautéed in butter may be sprinkled on top.

SALADE MIMOSA

Red beets　　　　　　　　　　*Boston lettuce*
Boiled eggs　　　　　　　　　*VINAIGRETTE DRESSING*

Cook the fresh beets in salted water. Cool and peel. Slice the beets and eggs. Place on top of the lettuce. Add the *VINAIGRETTE DRESSING*.

VINAIGRETTE DRESSING

2 *tablespoons mustard*　　　　1½ *cups oil*
6 *tablespoons red wine*　　　　*Salt and pepper, to taste*
　　vinegar

Mix the mustard with vinegar. Add the oil slowly, whisking vigorously, and season to taste.

Walnut, peanut or salad oil may be used.

FLOATING ISLAND

2 cups egg whites
1 quart milk
1 cup sugar

½ teaspoon vanilla extract
CRÈME ANGLAISE

1. Beat the egg whites until firm. Spoon the egg white to form a football shape. Cook 2 minutes on each side in hot (not boiling) milk with sugar and vanilla. Set aside.
2. When the "islands" are cool, pour *CRÈME ANGLAISE* over and serve.

CRÈME ANGLAISE

2 cups strained, hot milk
(use milk from Floating
Island recipe)

3 egg yolks

Mix the hot milk with the yolks. Put back on a slow fire, stirring constantly with a wooden spoon until it starts to thicken. Do not boil. Remove from the stove, and let cool down. Pour over the cool egg whites. (Do not overcook crème or it will curdle.)

A melted caramel should be added; drizzle it in a criss-cross pattern over the egg white before pouring the Crème Anglaise on top. You may garnish with seasonal red berries.

Creole Brunch for Six

Cream of Crawfish Soup

Eggs New Orleans

Sausage Stuffed Tomatoes

Breakfast Shrimp

Cheese Grits

Baking Powder Biscuits

Strawberry Crêpes

Beverages:

Orange Blossom Flip

Champagne

Coffee and Chicory

Dooky and Leah Chase, Proprietors

Leah Chase, Executive Chef

DOOKY CHASE'S

Dooky Chase's was established in 1941 by the late Edgar "Dooky" Chase, Sr. and his wife, Emily Tenette, who continues to be a vibrant force in the business. The walls of the restaurant's dining room are covered with beautiful art, a Kohlmeyer, a Brice, and many other noted names, but in the kitchen there is only one artist, Leah Chase. Born and educated in Louisiana, Leah learned how to cook in the kitchen of a small restaurant in the French Quarter.

Dooky Chase, Jr., a great local musician, married Leah and, after the death of his father, they took over the operation of the restaurant. Recently remodeled in rosy shades with beautifully furnished public rooms and two private dining rooms, the food remains as fantastic as it has been since 1941.

Leah is a unique lady. She walks into the restaurant beautifully dressed and coiffed, having just come from a meeting of one of the many boards she serves on—the symphony, the ballet, or the New Orleans Museum of Art. She greets most guests by name and then excuses herself to put on her "cooking clothes and shoes!"

Leah says, "I offer authentic Creole food." It's good food, and she is a great hostess. She looks around the restaurant and says, "I like it here because I'm at home."

Dooky Chase's is considered by many—both black and white—to be a New Orleans landmark and has received both local and national acclaim.

The restaurant offers "Creole style" catering and take out services in freezer packs. Leah says, "All my recipes are easy to make at home." Dooky Chase's is a must!

2301 Orleans Avenue

CREAM OF CRAWFISH SOUP

1 *pound cooked crawfish*
  tails
4 *tablespoons butter*
2 *tablespoons flour*
¼ *cup finely chopped onion*
2 *cups breakfast cream*

3 *cups water*
1 *teaspoon paprika*
½ *teaspoon cayenne pepper*
½ *teaspoon salt*
1 *teaspoon chopped parsley*

1. Put the crawfish tails in a blender and process until they are puréed; set aside.

2. Melt the butter; add the flour, stir, and cook for about 5 minutes, but do not brown. Add the onions and cook until the onions are tender. Add the puréed crawfish tails, stirring and cooking for 5 minutes. Slowly add the cream and water, stirring constantly; add the paprika, cayenne pepper, salt, and parsley. Cook slowly for 20 minutes on a slow flame.

Save six large crawfish in their shells to float on the soup.

EGGS NEW ORLEANS

1 *stick butter*
2 *tablespoons flour*
2 *cups evaporated milk*
1 *cup water*
½ *teaspoon salt*
⅓ *teaspoon cayenne pepper*
1 *teaspoon Worcestershire*
  sauce

1 *pound white crabmeat,*
  thoroughly picked over
6 *hard-boiled eggs*
  Paprika
1 *tablespoon chopped parsley*

1. Melt the butter in a pot, add the flour, stir well and cook about 5 minutes. Add the milk, slowly stirring constantly; add the water, cooking slowly until the mixture thickens. Add the salt, cayenne pepper, Worcestershire sauce, and crabmeat and cook for another 5 minutes. Pour into a pyrex dish.

2. Cut the eggs in half and place, cut side up, on the crabmeat mixture; sprinkle a little paprika and parsley over the top. Bake in an oven preheated to 375° for 10 minutes.

SAUSAGE STUFFED TOMATOES

6 medium sized ripe
   tomatoes
1½ pounds hot pork sausage
½ cup chopped onions
1 clove garlic, finely chopped
¼ cup chopped green
   bell peppers

1 teaspoon salt
½ teaspoon paprika
1 tablespoon chopped
   parsley
1 tablespoon butter
1½ cups breadcrumbs

1. Cut the stem end off the tomatoes and with a teaspoon scoop out and reserve the pulp; set the shells aside.

2. In a 2-quart saucepan, put the sausage meat, onions, garlic, bell peppers, salt, paprika, parsley, butter, and tomato pulp. Stir well. Cook until all ingredients are done, about 35 minutes on medium heat. When done, tighten the mixture with breadcrumbs.

3. Stuff the tomato shells full; sprinkle the tops with breadcrumbs. Warm the stuffed tomatoes in a 350° oven for 15 minutes.

This may be prepared the night before using.

BREAKFAST SHRIMP

4 tomatoes (very ripe)
1 stick butter
½ cup chopped onions
¼ cup chopped green bell
   peppers
2 cloves garlic, chopped finely
2 pounds shrimp, peeled
   and deveined

1 teaspoon paprika
½ teaspoon salt
¼ teaspoon cayenne pepper
1 tablespoon chopped parsley

1. Dip the tomatoes in boiling water, peel, and chop; set aside.

2. Melt the butter in a pot; add the onions, bell peppers, and garlic. Sauté until the onions are clear.

3. Add the tomatoes, shrimp, paprika, salt, and cayenne pepper. Sauté 10 minutes until the shrimp are done. Sprinkle parsley on top.

This may be served with rice, if desired.

CHEESE GRITS

4 cups water
1 cup quick grits

½ teaspoon salt
1 cup grated Cheddar cheese

1. Bring the water to a rolling boil; add the grits and salt and return to a boil. Reduce the heat and cook 2-4 minutes; add the grated cheese, stirring constantly until the cheese is completely melted.

2. Pour in a baking dish. Bake in an oven preheated to 350° for 5 minutes.

This is a wonderful, easy to make New Orleans dish.

BAKING POWDER BISCUITS

3 cups flour
4½ teaspoons baking powder
1¼ teaspoons salt

1 cup solid vegetable
   shortening
1½ cups milk

1. Sift the flour, baking powder, and salt together in a large bowl; cut in the shortening until the mixture is like coarse crumbs. Add the milk and stir until moist.

2. Place the dough on a floured board; knead a little to get the dough to hold. Roll out and cut. Place on an ungreased baking sheet in an oven preheated to 450°. Bake for about 20 minutes, until brown.

Serve with two or three different preserves.

STRAWBERRY CRÊPES

4 eggs
½ cup milk
½ cup water
2 tablespoons butter
2 tablespoons brandy
1 cup flour
½ teaspoon salt

1 tablespoon vanilla
2 tablespoons sugar
Melted butter
Powdered sugar
2 pints fresh sweetened
   strawberries
Whipped cream

1. Place the eggs, milk, water, 2 tablespoons butter, brandy, flour, salt, vanilla, and sugar in a blender. Blend until smooth. Let the batter stand at room temperature for 30 minutes.

2. Heat a 7" skillet; brush with melted butter. Pour in 2 tablespoons batter for each crêpe, turning and tilting the skillet to spread thin. Brown on one side.

3. Set all crêpes out on a warm platter and sprinkle each crêpe with powdered sugar. Place strawberries in the center of each crêpe, and fold, envelope fashion. Spoon a few strawberries on top. Garnish with whipped cream.

ORANGE BLOSSOM FLIP

1 *quart breakfast cream*
1 *pint orange juice*

1 *pint cream sherry*
Ice

Shake all ingredients with ice and serve immediately.

A Creole brunch is an experience all gourmets should enjoy at least once in their lives.

This entire menu is exciting, and Leah Chase loves to prepare it for people who come to the restaurant from all over the country.

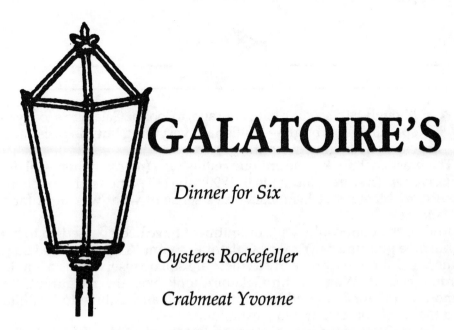

GALATOIRE'S

Dinner for Six

Oysters Rockefeller

Crabmeat Yvonne

Green Salad with Garlic Dressing Chapon

Crêpes Maison

Wines:

Pouligney Montrachet

Chateau Montelena Chardonnay

Yvonne Galatoire Wynne, President

Justin Galatoire Frey and David Gooch,
Vice Presidents and Co-Managers

Leon Galatoire, Assistant Manager

Charlie Plough, Chef

GALATOIRE'S

Although 1905 seems a long time ago, to look at Galatoire's today—sparkling and bright—it still has everything but the geese and chicken hanging in front.

The brass coat hooks, the antique ceiling fans (many of them still the originals which were handmade in 1890), the crisp linens, the excellent service are all signs of Jean Galatoire's sense of what was right for a restaurant.

And so the philosophy and commitment have been passed on to his handsome grandniece, Yvonne Galatoire Wynne. The great food continues, and the lines form early as there are still no reservations or credit cards accepted. When Justin Galatoire took over the restaurant, he announced that he wanted his brothers Leon and Gabriel to join him and the family of restaurateurs expanded.

Galatoire's is closed on holidays and Mondays. All other days the tables are filled, mostly with local people who have followed their parents and grandparents into the lines. Almost everyone knows each other and greetings continue throughout the meals.

Before World War II there was a major fire. Mr. Galatoire rallied everyone around him in order to clean up, restore, and reopen the doors. He accomplished this within two weeks.

Yvonne and her husband, attorney Robert Douglas Wynne who also devotes a great deal of his time to the welfare of the restaurant, head a family which brings great pleasure to natives and travelers alike.

209 Bourbon Street

OYSTERS ROCKEFELLER

4 dozen oysters
½ pound fresh spinach
1 bunch celery
1 bunch green onions
1 bunch anise
1 bunch parsley

1½ pounds butter, melted
¼ cup Worcestershire sauce
2 tablespoons absinthe
Salt, pepper, and cayenne
pepper

1. Parboil the oysters in their liquor until their edges curl.

2. Grind the vegetables very fine; add the melted butter to the vegetable paste.

3. Add the Worcestershire sauce; add the absinthe. Season with salt, pepper, and cayenne pepper to taste.

4. Dress each parboiled oyster on a shell; cover each oyster with one spoonful of stuffing.

5. Preheat the oven to 350°. Put the oysters under the broiler until they are brown and slightly crusty. Watch carefully not to let them burn.

This is a dish fit for a Rockefeller but also for everyone who enjoys good food.

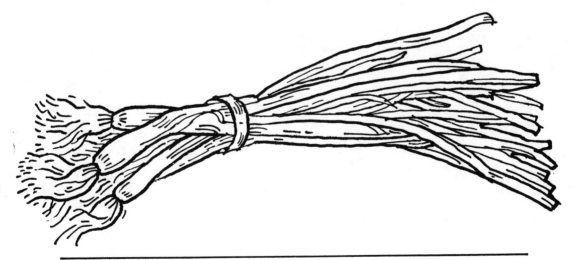

CRABMEAT YVONNE

6 *artichokes boiled (fresh preferred)*

1 *pound fresh mushrooms, sliced*

½ *cup clarified butter*

2 *pounds fresh backfin lump crabmeat, picked over*

Salt and white pepper, to taste

Chopped parsley, for garnish

Toast points

6 *lemon wedges, for garnish*

1. Boil the artichokes. When done, remove the leaves and the choke. Cut the bottoms into wedges.
2. Place the mushrooms in a large skillet; sauté in butter.
3. Add the artichoke bottoms and crabmeat. Sauté gently until heated thoroughly. Season with salt and white pepper.
4. Garnish with finely chopped parsley. Serve over toast points with a lemon wedge.

This recipe was named for a lovely lady of the family.

GREEN SALAD WITH GARLIC CHAPON DRESSING

1 *head lettuce*
1 *bunch watercress*
   Small amount of chicory

GARLIC CHAPON
DRESSING
French bread crust
Garlic

1. Toss all salad greens until thoroughly mixed. Refrigerate until crisp and cold before serving.
2. When ready to serve, toss the greens with *GARLIC CHAPON DRESSING.*
3. Cut the crust from a French bread in chunks; rub well with garlic and place over the salad.

GARLIC CHAPON DRESSING

1½ *tablespoons Creole mustard*
 ½ *cup vinegar*
 1 *tablespoon Worcestershire*
    sauce

1 *cup oil*
   Salt and pepper, to taste

Combine all ingredients. Shake vigorously before serving over the salad.

CRÊPES MAISON

8 tablespoons currant jelly	Peel of 1 orange and 1 lemon, slivered
12 (6-inch) BASIC CRÊPES	Powdered sugar
5 tablespoons toasted, sliced almonds	6 jiggers Grand Marnier, or to taste

1. Roll 1 tablespoon jelly in each crêpe.
2. Place 2 crêpes on each of six ovenproof plates. Top with sliced almonds, orange and lemon peel, and sprinkle with powdered sugar. Pass under the broiler until hot. Pour a jigger of Grand Marnier over each serving.

This is one of the best crêpe recipes you will find anywhere.

BASIC CRÊPES

3 tablespoons butter	½ cup water
3 eggs, slightly beaten	¾ cup all-purpose flour
½ cup milk	½ teaspoon salt

1. Melt the butter in 10-inch omelet pan (or 8-inch crêpe pan).

2. In a bowl, beat the eggs, milk, water, and melted butter together with a rotary beater. Blend in the flour and salt until mixture is smooth.

3. On medium-high, heat the buttered pan until just hot enough to sizzle a drop of water. For each crêpe pour a scant ¼ cup (2 tablespoons in an 8-inch pan) batter in the pan, rotating the pan as the batter is poured. Cook until lightly browned on the bottom; remove the crêpe from the pan or, if desired, turn and brown the other side. (Crêpes to be filled need to be browned on one side only. Use unbrowned side for filling.)

4. Stack between sheets of paper toweling or waxed paper until ready to use. Crêpes may be frozen. Makes approximately twelve 7½-inch crêpes or sixteen 6½-inch crêpes.

INDULGENCE

Dinner for Six

Shrimp with Herbsaint

Veal with Crawfish

Spinach and Belgian Endive
Salad with Warm Pecan and Tasso Vinaigrette

Frozen Mocha Pie

Wines:

Fumé Blanc

Fleurie Georges Du Boeuf

Elizabeth Page and Frank Bailey, Owners

Frank Bailey, Chef

INDULGENCE

E lizabeth "Liz" Page—a girl who loved to cook—became a gourmet chef by training at La Varenne and the Cordon Bleu in Paris. When she returned to her native New Orleans, she and Frank Bailey, a fine chef and food writer, joined forces and moved quickly into the board rooms of banks and corporations and into the dining rooms of fine homes by setting up and marketing an elegant catering service.

Gourmet food was produced in what had been a tiny grocery store at the corner of Orange and Religious Streets in the Irish Channel district. There was room for five tables in the front of the old building and Indulgence—a tiny but elegant restaurant—was born in that front room.

It took Liz and Frank only a short time to develop their unique interpretations of Louisiana's culinary presentations. Now four years old, their contemporary Creole cuisine, an innovative and subtle rendition of New Orleans' famous food, has resulted in Indulgence being recognized as an established fine restaurant.

Five tables soon were not enough to take care of the crowds who sought Indulgence, and a larger location was added in the Garden District, where Page and Bailey are hitting their stride as tastemakers in a city known around the world for outstanding restaurants. It is even rumored that a second floor will soon be added with the name "Over Indulgence"!

The sample menu showcases the creativity of Indulgence with the rich bounty of Louisiana's waters, forests, and farms, prepared with classic and modern techniques.

1501 Washington Avenue

SHRIMP WITH HERBSAINT

2 dozen large shrimp,
   peeled and deveined
2 tablespoons butter
1 tablespoon minced garlic
3 tablespoons minced
   shallots
¼ cup Herbsaint (or Pernod)

½ cup heavy cream
2 tablespoons fresh dill or
   1 tablespoon dried
   dill weed
¼ cup minced flat parsley
Salt and pepper

1. Allow the shrimp to come to room temperature.

2. Melt the butter in a large pan and add the shrimp, garlic, and shallots. Cook and toss over moderate heat for 5-6 minutes.

3. Carefully add the Herbsaint and flambé. When the flames subside, remove the shrimp with a slotted spoon.

4. Add the cream and herbs. Reduce by one-third. Add the reserved shrimp to heat through. Serve in a gratin dish.

"Not Creole, but just plain New Orleans," Liz says.

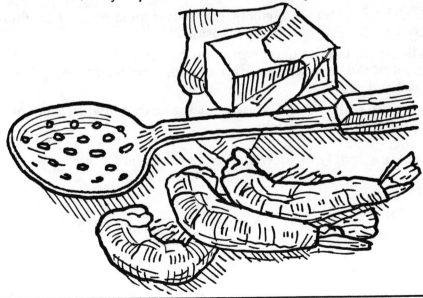

VEAL WITH CRAWFISH

6 (4-ounce) veal scallops,
    pounded thin
Flour
Salt and pepper
Peanut oil
¼ cup white wine
1 can Italian plum
    tomatoes, juice reserved,
    tomatoes chopped

1 pound crawfish tails (or
    shrimp), raw, peeled and
    deveined
3 tablespoons chopped
    shallots
1 tablespoon minced garlic
1 orange
½ tablespoon each of
    oregano, thyme,
    marjoram, and sage

1. Dust the scallops lightly with flour, salt, and pepper and sauté in peanut oil for 2 or 3 minutes on each side.

2. Remove from the pan and keep warm. Pour off remaining oil and return the pan to the stove. Immediately add the white wine and juice from the tomatoes. Scrape the pan vigorously to dislodge all particles from the bottom of the pan. Let the wine and juice reduce to half.

3. Add the crawfish tails, shallots, garlic, and tomatoes and continue to cook for 5 minutes, stirring occasionally.

4. Grate the rind of the orange into the pan and then squeeze in the juice. Add the herbs and cook for an additional 5 minutes and taste for salt and pepper.

5. Place 1 veal scallop on each dinner plate and the crawfish sauce over the veal. Serve immediately.

This is a wonderful entrée for dinner or for an elegant luncheon.

SPINACH AND BELGIAN ENDIVE SALAD WITH WARM PECAN AND TASSO VINAIGRETTE

1 *pound fresh spinach*
2 *Belgian endive*

PECAN AND TASSO VINAIGRETTE

1. Clean the spinach of all stains; wash thoroughly and dry completely. Cut the endive in thin, crosswise slices. Place the greens in a metal bowl.
2. Prepare the *PECAN AND TASSO VINAIGRETTE*. Pour the boiling dressing over the greens, toss quickly, and serve at once.

PECAN AND TASSO VINAIGRETTE

4 *tablespoons unsalted butter*
1 *cup pecan pieces*
6 *tablespoons tasso, cut into tiny pieces*
¼ *cup red wine vinegar*

2 *tablespoons walnut oil*
1 *tablespoon chopped shallots*
1 *teaspoon chopped garlic*
½ *cup olive oil*

1. In a medium size sauté pan, place the butter and pecans. Cook to warm the pecans and toast them lightly.
2. Add the tasso, vinegar, walnut oil, shallots, garlic, and olive oil. Bring to a boil and pour over the greens.

Tasso is a highly seasoned ham developed in Louisiana's Cajun country.

FROZEN MOCHA PIE

CRUST:

1	cup flour, sifted
⅓	cup light brown sugar, firmly packed
4	tablespoons chilled butter
2	tablespoons chilled shortening
¾	cup pecan pieces
1	ounce grated unsweetened chocolate
1	teaspoon vanilla
2	tablespoons cold water

FILLING:

12	tablespoons butter
1	cup light brown sugar, firmly packed
1½	ounces unsweetened chocolate, melted
1	tablespoon instant chicory coffee
3	eggs

TOPPING:

2	cups heavy cream
½	cup powdered sugar
¼	cup dark rum

1. To make the *CRUST,* preheat the oven to 375°. Combine the flour and sugar in a bowl. Cut the butter and shortening into the flour with a fork until of a mealy consistency. Add the pecans and chocolate. Add the vanilla and water. Press into a lightly greased 9-inch pan. Bake 12-15 minutes, remove from the oven, and cool.

2. To make the *FILLING,* cream the butter and sugar together until light and creamy (about 5 minutes). Add the chocolate and coffee to the creamed butter. Continue beating and add the eggs, one at a time, at 2 minute intervals. Pour the mixture into the cooled crust and refrigerate for 6 hours, or until set.

3. To make the Topping, whip the cream with the sugar and rum until firm. Place the topping over the filling and freeze until ready to serve.

If wrapped well, the pie will keep in the freezer up to one week.

NEW ORLEANS

JONATHAN

A RESTAURANT

Dinner for Six

Trout Mousse

Angels on Horseback

Iced Cream of Watercress Soup

Chef's Yeast Rolls

Tenderloin of Pork Cordon Bleu

Barbados Rum Trifle

Cappucino Dell' Amore

Wines:

With the First Courses—Calloway Fumé Blanc

With the Pork—A young Beaujolais

Michael Morris, Proprietor

Tom Cowman, Executive Chef

JONATHAN

Jonathan is one of the most exquisite restaurants in this area. Some of the most famous artists are represented in the restaurant. Erté—the master of Art Deco—has his fine hand on all three floors of this old building. Dennis Abbé is responsible for the mural in the front hall which sets the tone. The artistry extends to the kitchen.

Michael Morris, the owner, and Tom Cowman, Executive Chef, are a team which provides a top menu with a taste of the highest caliber.

Chef Cowman says that one must "save space" for the delicious desserts. The wine list at Jonathan has been commended for its versatility as well as for its modest price.

The restaurant is across from Armstrong Park and the Theatre of the Performing Arts, so that very often special dinners are arranged for the stars and their admirers. Theatre and concert goers are attracted to Jonathan, which is open every day until 11:00 PM.

Chef Cowman's early talents lay in the field of advertising, but cooking overcame that bent. When he opened his own restaurant in the Hamptons, Craig Claiborne of *The New York Times* gave it three stars and listed it as one of his 100 favorite restaurants in the whole world!

When asked what brought him to New Orleans, Chef Cowman exclaimed, as have so many, "This is the capital of food in the United States." Restaurant Jonathan received the Mobil and Travel Holiday awards for seven consecutive years. Michael and Tom describe the restaurant as inter-continental with a creole flavor.

For your convenience, valet parking is available.

714 North Rampart Street

TROUT MOUSSE

1 quart water
1 cup dry sherry
1 onion, roughly chopped
1 bay leaf
3 stalks celery
½ teaspoon plus a pinch of
  white pepper
  Salt
3 tablespoons plain gelatin
1 pound boned trout fillets
6 egg whites, reserve
  shells
1 cup mayonnaise
1 tablespoon lemon juice
2 tablespoons Dijon mustard

½ teaspoon tarragon leaf
  (crushed)
1½ tablespoons dill weed
1 tablespoon onion powder
2 tablespoons tarragon
  vinegar
Black olives
Pimiento
Dill leaves (if available)
Lemon, for garnish
Parsley, for garnish
Cherry tomatoes,
  for garnish
DILL MAYONNAISE

1. To make the stock, place the water, sherry, onion, bay leaf, celery, pinch of white pepper, salt to taste, and 2 tablespoons plain gelatin in a saucepan and bring to a full boil for 15 minutes or more.

2. In a pot, put the pound tròut fillets (flounder or sole may be used instead of trout) and strain the stock through cheesecloth over the fish; on low flame let it simmer for a few minutes until the fish flakes (do not overcook). Strain the contents of pot through a cheesecloth into another pot, putting the fish plus 1 cup of stock in a bowl over ice. While the fish is cooling, clarify the stock to make a clear aspic.

3. To clarify the stock, put 6 egg whites and shells into the stock; bring to a boil, stirring once, then remove from the fire. Skim, then strain through a cheesecloth. Let cool.

4. To make the mousse, in a bowl with the fish, whip in the mayonnaise, lemon juice, mustard, tarragon leaf, dill weed, ½ teaspoon white pepper and onion powder. (Mixture should have a smooth, light texture.) Add 1 tablespoon gelatin which has been dissolved in 2 tablespoons tarragon vinegar.

5. To assemble, pour ¼ inch aspic into a mold and let firm slightly; decorate with black olives, pimiento, and dill leaves. Carefully pour more aspic and let chill to firm. When firm, fill the mold with the fish mixture, wrap with plastic wrap, and place in the refrigerator to firm. When firm, remove from the mold by placing the mold into warm water for a few seconds, then by running a knife along the edge and inverting the mold onto a plate.

6. Garnish with lemon, parsley, and cherry tomatoes and serve with *DILL MAYONNAISE.*

DILL MAYONNAISE

2 cups mayonnaise	1 tablespoon Dijon mustard
2 tablespoons dill weed	1 teaspoon onion powder
1 raw egg yolk	Juice of 1 lemon
2 tablespoons dill vinegar (or substitute white vinegar)	Tabasco sauce, to taste

Mix the mayonnaise, dill weed, egg yolk, dill vinegar, Dijon mustard, onion powder, lemon juice, and a few drops of Tabasco.

Trout Mousse is a favorite at Jonathan's and could be stuffed in snow peas, cherry tomatoes or used for cocktail sandwiches.

ANGELS ON HORSEBACK

18 slices bacon	Rice flour
30-36 oysters	Melted butter
6 rounds of white bread	Lemon wedges
GARLIC BUTTER SAUCE	Parsley, for garnish

1. For each "Angel" parboil ½ piece bacon. Figure 5 to 6 oysters per person. Wrap an oyster with the bacon and secure with a toothpick; cut a round of bread for each serving and brush with *GARLIC BUTTER SAUCE*; place the rounds on a cookie sheet and bake at 350° until golden crisp.

2. When ready to serve, roll the angels in rice flour and deep fry until crisp (or bake in the oven); put the garlic rounds on a plate, stick the angels on the rounds and pour some of the melted butter over the angels. Garnish with a wedge of lemon and a sprig of parsley.

Angels make a wonderful hors d'oeuvre at a cocktail party.

GARLIC BUTTER SAUCE

¼ pound butter	Dash of fresh thyme, chopped
1 clove garlic, minced	
2 shallots, chopped	1 lemon
1 bunch fresh parsley, chopped	Cracked black pepper
	Tabasco sauce
1 teaspoon chopped, fresh chives	Worcestershire sauce
	Salt

Melt the butter; add the garlic, shallots, parsley, chives, thyme, lemon juice, pinch of cracked pepper, a good dash of Tabasco, a good dash of Worcestershire and salt to taste.

ICED CREAM OF WATERCRESS SOUP

2 Idaho potatoes, peeled and
  sliced
2 leeks, washed (whites
  only) cut in half
2 stalks celery
1 small onion, quartered
2 bay leaves
½ carrot

Rich chicken stock*
2 bunches watercress
½ quart heavy cream
½ quart half and half
  Salt
  Cayenne pepper

1. In a heavy pot put the potatoes, leeks, celery, onion, bay leaves, and carrot.

2. Cover with a rich chicken stock and bring to a boil. Cook until the vegetables are soft. Remove from the heat and cool. Remove the celery, carrot, and bay leaf. When cool, blend, and pass through a strainer.

3. While the above is cooking, remove the stems from the watercress. Cook the leaves for 2 minutes, or until wilted, in a little chicken stock. Cool and blend.

4. Mix the watercress into the potato and leek mixture. Add the heavy cream, half and half, salt to taste, and a good dash of cayenne pepper.

5. Refrigerate until very cold and serve in chilled soup cups or bowls.

*Use one can of chicken broth, or use your own recipe.

Possible substitutes for watercress are spinach, puréed red or green bell pepper, sorrel, or your own imagination.

JONATHAN

CHEF'S YEAST ROLLS

1 tablespoon sugar
1 teaspoon salt
¼ cup lard
1 tablespoon butter
1 cup boiling water
2 eggs
1 package instant yeast

1 cup lukewarm water
10 cups or more all-purpose flour
Melted butter
½ cup milk
Poppy seeds or sesame seeds

1. In a stainless steel bowl or glass crock, dissolve the sugar, salt, lard, and butter in the boiling water; allow to cool to body temperature and whisk in 1 egg.

2. Dissolve the instant yeast in the lukewarm (not hot-not cold) water; add a sprinkle of sugar.

3. Let rest for a moment until the yeast activates, then stir into the other liquid. Sift into the bowl 10 cups of flour and knead until the dough is elastic and smooth—adding more flour if necessary. Pour a little melted butter over the dough so it won't dry out and put it in a warm place to rise. In about 1½ hours, punch down and pinch off the rolls, putting them into muffin tins that have been greased with melted lard. Brush tops with 1 egg mixed in milk. Pinching three small balls (size of a large marble) makes clover leaf rolls. After brushing with egg and milk, sprinkle with poppy seeds or sesame seeds or leave plain. Let rise 1 hour and bake in 425° oven 10-12 minutes or until light golden brown.

These yeast rolls are another specialty at Jonathan. Use the rolls for break-fast, or you may slice and toast them for croutons.

This recipe makes approximately 2 dozen rolls.

TENDERLOIN OF PORK CORDON BLEU

2-3 tenderloins of pork
½ pound prosciutto ham
1 pound sliced Swiss cheese
2 tablespoons Dijon mustard
1 cup flour, seasoned with
    pinch of salt, white
    pepper, dry mustard,
    paprika, powdered
    thyme and
    onion powder
1 egg
1 cup milk

Breadcrumbs
2 tablespoons Romano cheese
1 chicken bouillon cube
1 tablespoon minced shallot
½ cup dry sherry
3 cups heavy cream
1 tablespoon crushed green
    peppercorns
Salt
Butter
Watercress, for garnish

1. Slice the tenderloin at an angle into ½ inch pieces—four per serving. You will need probably 2 tenderloins or 3 if small. Butterfly (split but do not cut all the way) the pieces and flatten with a mallet or side of heavy knife. Put aside.

2. Slice the prosciutto ham as thin as possible. Slice the Swiss cheese. Lay the pork out and brush one side with 1 tablespoon Dijon mustard; put the prosciutto and cheese between two pieces of pork. Pat the pork with seasoned flour; dip into egg wash (1 egg mixed with 1 cup milk); coat with breadcrumbs that have been mixed with grated Romano cheese. Refrigerate until ready to cook.

3. To prepare the green peppercorn sauce, in a heavy saucepan dissolve the chicken bouillon cube, minced shallot, dry sherry, and heavy cream. Reduce by cooking over high heat to 1½ cups liquid. Stir in 1 tablespoon Dijon mustard, crushed green peppercorns, and salt to taste. The sauce should be creamy but not thin. If thin, reduce some more.

4. To serve, sauté the pork tenders in butter, being careful not to scorch, until golden. Put them in a 350° oven for 15 to 20 minutes or

until done to preference. Put 2 slices of pork on one side of the plate, then put a line of the sauce along one side of the meat. Garnish with watercress.

Broccoli, a grilled tomato, and a tiny roast potato are very good with this.

This recipe may be used with chicken breasts or panée veal. The green peppercorn sauce is especially good on fish, particularly a firm fish—sword or red snapper.

BARBADOS RUM TRIFLE

2 cups half and half	1 cup milk
2 cups heavy cream	1 pineapple, peeled, cored and cubed
2 cups sugar	
¾ cup cornstarch	2 oranges, peeled and sectioned
1 tablespoon plus ½ teaspoon vanilla	2 bananas, sliced
6 tablepoons Barbados rum	2 cups seeded grapes
7 eggs	2 cups strawberries
1 cup plus 1 tablespoon butter	Lime juice
	Grated coconut
1 teaspoon almond extract	Raspberry jam
3 cups cake flour	Whipped cream
1 tablespoon baking powder	Slivered almonds
Salt	

1. To make the custard, in a double boiler heat the half and half, heavy cream, and 1 cup sugar. When hot, whisk in ¾ cup cornstarch which has been dissolved in 1 tablespoon vanilla and 2 tablespoons Barbados rum. Stir for 10 to 15 minutes or until the cornstarch taste disappears. Add 4 egg yolks (save the whites) and whisk for 5 minutes more. Remove from the heat and stir in 1 tablespoon butter.

2. To make the almond cake, mix 1 cup butter, 1 cup sugar, 1 teaspoon almond extract, ½ teaspoon vanilla, and 3 egg yolks (save the whites). Then sift the cake flour, baking powder, and pinch of salt. Then, alternating (starting and ending with the flour), add the flour mixture and the milk. Whip 6 egg whites until stiff, fold into the mixture, and put into three 9-inch cake pans with bottoms that have been greased and dusted with flour. Bake at 350° until done, approximately 30 minutes. Cool, then remove to cake racks to cool. (Any pre-baked cake, except chocolate, can be used in this recipe. "Store bought" pound cake is good.)

3. To prepare the fruit, put into a bowl the pineapple, oranges, bananas, seeded grapes, and strawberries. Sprinkle with lime juice and 1 teaspoon Barbados rum.

4. To assemble, if you have a straight sided bowl it is best, especially if the dessert is to be presented. In the bottom of the bowl, put a layer of cake. Sprinkle with the lime and Barbados rum*, add a layer of custard, then the fruit. At this point press slices of oranges and half strawberries against the side of the bowl. Continue to add cake, rum, custard, and fruit, ending up with custard on top. Sprinkle coconut over the top and dot with raspberry jam and a strawberry in the center. When serving, dig down through the layers. Serve with whipped cream and sprinkle of almonds.

*Rum should be added to taste in each layer.

CAPPUCINO DELL' AMORE

At least one day ahead, make the base for this after-dinner drink. The longer it sits, the better.

Put into a bottle equal parts of:

Brandy
Gin
Rum
Galliano
White Crème de Cocoa
Dark Crème de Cocoa
2 or 3 cinnamon sticks
4 or 5 cloves

When ready to serve, put a good 2 ounces in the cappucino mug or coffee cup and fill with cappucino (espresso coffee, grated unsweetened chocolate, sugar, and hot half and half).

Top with whipped cream, a sprinkle of almonds and shaved unsweetened chocolate.

Some options for this recipe include making iced espresso or using it as a topping for coffee ice cream.

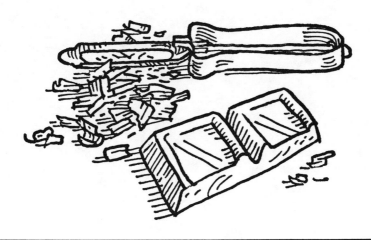

K-PAUL'S LOUISIANA KITCHEN

Dinner for Six

Cajun Popcorn with Sherry Wine Sauce

Chicken and Andouille Smoked Sausage Gumbo

Blackened Redfish

Corn Maque Choux

Mashed Potatoes

Sweet Potato Pecan Pie with Chantilly Cream

Beverages:

Cajun Martini

Dixie Beer

Cartlidge and Brown Chardonnay, 1983

New Orleans Coffee and Chicory

K and Paul Prudhomme, Proprietors

Paul Prudhomme, Chef

K-PAUL'S

C hef Paul Prudhomme says it took him years to learn two crucial things about food and restaurants: first, it's worth every bit of effort and money to serve the freshest ingredients you can possibly find—"It just makes all the difference in the world!", and second, it pays to put all of your energy into serving the very best quality food imaginable—and never to settle for less. Chef Paul says, "I'm lucky! I have my own restaurant, K-Paul's Louisiana Kitchen, and I can do both of these things. I put all the money on the plate, and I keep the restaurant small enough to ensure complete quality control of everything we prepare."

Chef Paul's wife, K, and Chef Paul opened K-Paul's in the summer of 1979. Chef Paul is a Cajun and the restaurant reflects his memory of Cajun restaurants from his youth. As Chef Paul puts it, "It's definitely homey, and that's what I want, since Cajun cooking is really *home* cooking." K-Paul's started out with just one cook and one waitress and, without any advertising or promotion, became so popular that it quickly grew to be a very well staffed restaurant that serves many complex dishes.

K-Paul's menu changes daily according to what fresh foods are available from purveyors. Local products are used almost exclusively because Louisiana is blessed with such a wealth of wildlife, freshwater and saltwater fish and other seafoods, and fruits and vegetables.

The style of food served at K-Paul's is the end result of many influences according to Chef Paul: "my Cajun heritage (I learned to cook at my mother's side starting at age seven), my years in New Orleans learning Creole cooking, my work with chefs and cooks around the country learning the different regional cuisines, and, finally, the refining of all this into my own style—which continues to change as I experiment and learn and grow."

K-Paul's has a wonderful, fun-loving feel to it, and the waitresses certainly promote this special feeling. And the cooking staff is tops, the finest; they, just as is Chef Paul, are committed to making every bite of food served an instant joy as well as a memorable experience.

The world famous chef says, "I'm really proud of K-Paul's and our high standards for fresh, best quality products prepared in a distinctive Louisiana way. Our food makes you happy!"

416 Chartres Street

CAJUN POPCORN WITH SHERRY WINE SAUCE

2 *eggs, well beaten*
1¼ *cups milk*
½ *cup corn flour**
½ *cup all-purpose flour*
1 *teaspoon sugar*
1 *teaspoon salt*
½ *teaspoon onion powder*
½ *teaspoon garlic powder*
½ *teaspoon white pepper*
½ *teaspoon ground red pepper (preferably cayenne)*

¼ *teaspoon dried thyme leaves*
⅛ *teaspoon dried sweet basil leaves*
⅛ *teaspoon black pepper Vegetable oil, for deep frying*
2 *pounds peeled crawfish tails, small shrimp, or lump crabmeat (picked over)*
SHERRY WINE SAUCE

1. Combine the eggs and milk in a small bowl, blending well.
2. In a large bowl combine the flours, sugar, and seasonings, mixing well. Add half of the egg mixture and whisk until well blended, then thoroughly blend in the remaining egg mixture. Let sit 1 hour at room temperature (to let the flour expand).
3. Heat 1 inch oil in a large skillet or deep fryer to 370°. Coat the seafood with the batter and fry in batches in the hot oil until golden brown on both sides, about 2 minutes total, turning once or twice while cooking. (Adjust heat to maintain oil's temperature as close to 370° as possible.) Drain on paper towels. Serve immediately with *SHERRY WINE SAUCE* on the side.

Makes 12 appetizer servings (or 6 Cajun servings).

**Corn flour is available at many health food stores and is recommended. If not available, substitute all-purpose flour.*

It's very important to cook this as quickly as possible and not below 350°, so the seafood will be crisp but not overcooked.

SHERRY WINE SAUCE

1 egg yolk
¼ cup catsup
3 tablespoons finely
  chopped green onions
2 tablespoons dry sherry
1 teaspoon Creole mustard
  (preferred) or brown
  mustard

¼ teaspoon salt
¼ teaspoon white pepper
¼ teaspoon Tabasco sauce
½ cup vegetable oil

Place all ingredients except the oil in a food processor or blender; process about 30 seconds. With the machine still running, add the oil in a thin, steady stream; continue processing until smooth, about 1 minute, pushing the sides down once with a rubber spatula.

Makes about 1 cup.

Copyright© 1984 by Paul Prudhomme

CHICKEN AND ANDOUILLE SMOKED SAUSAGE GUMBO

1 (2- to 3-pound) chicken,
  cut up
  Salt
  Garlic powder
  Ground red pepper
  (preferably cayenne)
1 cup finely chopped onions
1 cup finely chopped green
  bell peppers
¾ cup finely chopped celery
1¼ cups all-purpose flour
½ teaspoon salt

½ teaspoon garlic powder
½ teaspoon ground red
  pepper (preferably
  cayenne)
  Vegetable oil for deep
  frying
  About 7 cups BASIC
  CHICKEN STOCK
½ pound andouille smoked
  sausage, cut into ¼-inch
  cubes
1 teaspoon minced garlic
  Hot BASIC COOKED RICE

1. Remove excess fat from the chicken pieces. Rub a generous amount of salt, garlic powder, and red pepper on both sides of each piece,

making sure each is evenly covered. Let stand at room temperature for 30 minutes.

2. Meanwhile, in a medium-size bowl combine the onions, bell peppers, and celery; set aside.

3. Combine the flour, the ½ teaspoon salt, ½ teaspoon garlic powder, and ½ teaspoon red pepper in a paper or plastic bag. Add the chicken pieces and shake until chicken is well coated. Reserve ½ cup of the seasoned flour.

4. In a large heavy skillet (preferably not a nonstick type), heat 1½ inches of oil until very hot (375° to 400°). Fry chicken until the crust is brown on both sides and meat is cooked, about 5 to 8 minutes per side; drain on paper towels. Carefully pour the hot oil into a glass measuring cup, leaving as many of the browned particles in the pan as possible. Scrape the pan bottom with a metal whisk to loosen any stuck particles, then return ½ cup of the hot oil to the pan.

5. Place pan over high heat. Using a long- handled metal whisk, gradually stir in the reserved ½ cup flour. Cook, whisking constantly, until the roux is dark red-brown to black, about 3½ to 4 minutes, being careful not to let it scorch or splash on your skin. Remove from heat and immediately add the reserved vegetable mixture, stirring constantly until the roux stops getting darker. Return pan to low heat and cook until vegetables are soft, about 5 minutes, stirring constantly and scraping the pan bottom well.

6. Place the *BASIC CHICKEN STOCK* in a 5½ quart saucepan or large Dutch oven. Bring to a boil. Add roux mixture by spoonfuls to the boiling stock, stirring until dissolved between each addition. Return to a boil, stirring and scraping the pan bottom often. Reduce the heat to a simmer and stir in the andouille and minced garlic. Simmer uncovered for about 45 minutes, stirring often toward the end of cooking time.

7. While the gumbo is simmering, debone the cooked chicken and dice the meat into ½-inch pieces. When the gumbo is cooked, stir in the

chicken and adjust seasoning with salt and pepper. Serve immediately.

8. To serve as a main course, mound ⅓ cup cooked rice in the center of a soup bowl; ladle about 1¼ cups gumbo around the rice. For an appetizer, place 1 heaping teaspoon cooked rice in a cup and ladle about ¾ cup gumbo on top.

This recipe makes 6 main-dish or 10 appetizer servings and is super with potato salad served on the side.

Any good, pure smoked pork sausage such as Polish sausage (Kielbasa) may be substituted for andouille.

Copyright © 1984 by Paul Prudhomme

BASIC COOKED RICE

2 cups uncooked rice (preferably converted)
2½ cups BASIC CHICKEN STOCK
1½ tablespoons very finely chopped onions
1½ tablespoons very finely chopped celery
1½ tablespoons very finely chopped green bell peppers

1½ tablespoons unsalted butter (preferred) or margarine, melted
½ teaspoon salt
⅛ teaspoon garlic powder
A pinch each of white pepper, ground red pepper (preferably cayenne) and black pepper

In a 5x9x2½-inch loaf pan, combine all ingredients; mix well. Seal pan snugly with aluminum foil. Bake at 350° until the rice is tender, about 1 hour, 10 minutes. Serve immediately.

Makes 6 cups.

If you make this ahead of time and store it, omit the bell peppers as they tend to sour quickly.

Copyright © 1984 by Paul Prudhomme

BASIC BEEF, PORK OR CHICKEN STOCK

About 2 quarts cold water*
1 *medium onion, unpeeled*
   and quartered
1 *rib celery*
1 *large clove garlic,*
   unpeeled and quartered

1½ to 2 pounds beef shank (preferred) or other beef bones, or 1½ to 2 pounds pork neck bones (preferred) or other pork bones, or 1½ to 2 pounds chicken backs, necks, giblets (excluding liver) and/or bones

1. Place all ingredients in a large saucepan; bring to a boil over high heat, then gently simmer at least 4 hours, preferably 8 (unless otherwise directed in a recipe), replenishing the water as needed to keep about 1 quart of liquid in the pan. Strain, cool and refrigerate until ready to use. (<u>Note</u>: Remember, if you are short on time, that using a stock simmered 20 to 30 minutes is far better than using just water in any recipe.)

2. *TO MAKE A RICH STOCK:* Strain the Basic Stock, then continue simmering it until evaporation reduces the liquid by half or more. For example, if your recipe calls for 1 cup of Rich Stock, start it with at least 2 cups of strained Basic Stock. (Rich stocks are needed when a sauce requires lots of taste but only a limited amount of liquid. They are also excellent for general use.)

Makes 1 quart.

*Always start with cold water, enough to cover the other stock ingredients.

You can use the vegetable trimmings (onions and celery—not green bell pepper) from the recipe you are preparing.

Chef Paul has recently marketed his famous seasonings and named them Cajun Magic. *They are available in seven varieties: Poultry, Blackened Redfish, Seafood, Blackened Steak, Pork and Veal, Vegetable, and Meat.*

Copyright © 1984 by Paul Prudhomme

❦

K-PAUL'S

BLACKENED REDFISH

¾ pound (3 sticks) unsalted butter, melted in a skillet

1 tablespoon sweet paprika

2½ teaspoons salt

1 teaspoon onion powder

1 teaspoon garlic powder

1 teaspoon ground red pepper (preferably cayenne)

¾ teaspoon white pepper

¾ teaspoon black pepper

½ teaspoon dried thyme leaves

½ teaspoon dried oregano leaves

6 (8- to 10-ounce) fish fillets (preferably red-fish, pompano or tilefish), cut about ½-inch thick*

1. Heat a large cast iron skillet over very high heat until it is beyond the smoking stage and you see white ash in the skillet bottom (the skillet cannot be too hot for this dish), at least 10 minutes.

2. Meanwhile, pour 2 tablespoons melted butter in each of 6 small ramekins; set aside and keep warm. Reserve the remaining butter in its skillet. Heat the serving plates in a 250° oven.

3. Thoroughly combine all seasoning ingredients in a small bowl. Dip each fillet in the reserved melted butter so that both sides are well coated; then sprinkle the seasoning mix generously and evenly on both sides of the fillets, patting it in by hand. Place in the hot skillet and pour 1 teaspoon melted butter on top of each fillet (be careful as the butter may flame up). Cook uncovered over high heat until the underside looks charred, about 2 minutes (the time will vary according to the fillet's thickness and the heat of the skillet). Turn the fish over and pour 1 teaspoon more butter on top; cook until fish is done, about 2 minutes more. Repeat with remaining fillets. Serve each fillet while piping hot.

4. To serve, place one fillet and a ramekin of butter on each heated serving plate.

WARNING—COOKING METHOD PRODUCES INTENSE SMOKE; BEST COOKED OUTDOORS.

* Redfish and pompano are ideal for this method of cooking. If tilefish is used, you may have to split the fillets in half horizontally to have the proper thickness. If you can't get any of these fish, salmon steaks or red snapper fillets can be substituted. In any case, the fillets or steaks must not be more than ¾-inch thick.

This is the real thing created by Chef Paul and now being copied across the country. Follow this recipe carefully.

Copyright © 1984 by Paul Prudhomme

CORN MAQUE CHOUX

4 tablespoons unsalted butter	½ teaspoon salt
¼ cup vegetable oil	½ teaspoon ground red pepper (preferably cayenne)
7 cups fresh corn (about seventeen 8-inch cobs)	2½ cups BASIC CHICKEN, BEEF OR PORK STOCK (see page 123)
1 cup very finely chopped onions	4 tablespoons margarine
¼ cup sugar	1 cup evaporated milk
1 teaspoon white pepper	2 eggs

1. In a large skillet combine the butter and oil with the corn, onions, sugar, white pepper, salt, and red pepper. Cook over high heat until corn is tender and starch starts to form a crust on the pan bottom, about 12 to 14 minutes, stirring occasionally, and stirring more as mixture starts sticking. Gradually stir in 1 cup of the stock, scraping the pan bottom to remove crust as you stir. Continue cooking 5 minutes, stirring occasionally. Add the margarine, stir until melted and cook about 5 minutes, stirring frequently and scraping pan bottom

as needed. Reduce heat to low and cook about 10 minutes, stirring occasionally, then add ¼ cup additional stock and cook about 15 minutes, stirring fairly frequently. Add the remaining 1 cup stock and cook about 10 minutes, stirring occasionally. Stir in ½ cup of the milk and continue cooking until most of the liquid is absorbed, about 5 minutes, stirring occasionally. Remove from heat.

2. In a bowl combine the eggs and the remaining ½ cup milk; beat with a metal whisk until very frothy, about 1 minute. Add to the corn, stirring well. Serve immediately, allowing about ½ cup per person.

Makes 10 to 12 side-dish servings (or 6 Cajun servings).

Paul says his mother cooked a lot of sweet or semisweet dishes. One of these was Corn Maque Choux, which they ate with rice and gravy. Every Cajun family has its own recipe for Corn Maque Choux.

Copyright © 1984 by Paul Prudhomme

MASHED POTATOES

2 pounds white potatoes, peeled and quartered	½ pound (2 sticks) unsalted butter
¾ cup evaporated milk	1 teaspoon salt
	1 teaspoon white pepper

1. Boil the potatoes until fork-tender. Drain while still hot, reserving 1 cup water.

2. Place the hot potatoes in a large bowl with the milk, butter, salt and white pepper. Stir with a wooden spoon until broken up, then beat with a metal whisk (or electric mixer with a paddle) until creamy and smooth. (If the potatoes are not velvety creamy, mix in up to 1 cup of the reserved water.) Serve immediately.

Copyright © 1984 by Paul Prudhomme

SWEET POTATO PECAN PIE

DOUGH:
- 3 tablespoons unsalted butter, softened
- 2 tablespoons sugar
- ¼ teaspoon salt
- ½ of a whole egg, vigorously beaten until frothy (reserve the other half for the sweet-potato filling)
- 2 tablespoons cold milk
- 1 cup all-purpose flour

SWEET POTATO FILLING:
- 2-3 sweet potatoes (or enough to yield 1 cup cooked pulp), baked
- ¼ cup packed light brown sugar
- 2 tablespoons sugar
- ½ egg, vigorously beaten until frothy (reserved from above)
- 1 tablespoon heavy cream

- 1 tablespoon unsalted butter, softened
- 1 tablespoon vanilla extract
- ¼ teaspoon salt
- ¼ teaspoon ground cinnamon
- ⅛ teaspoon ground allspice
- ⅛ teaspoon ground nutmeg

PECAN PIE SYRUP:
- ¾ cup sugar
- ¾ cup dark corn syrup
- 2 small eggs
- 1½ tablespoons unsalted butter, melted
- 2 teaspoons vanilla extract
- Pinch of salt
- Pinch of ground cinnamon
- ¾ cup pecan pieces or halves
- *CHANTILLY CREAM*

1. To make the *DOUGH*, place the softened butter, sugar, and salt in the bowl of an electric mixer; beat on high speed until the mixture is creamy. Add the ½ egg and beat 30 seconds. Add the milk and beat on high speed 2 minutes. Add the flour and beat on medium speed 5 seconds, then on high speed just until blended, about 5 seconds more (over-mixing will produce a tough dough). Remove the dough from the bowl and shape into a 5-inch patty about ½-inch thick. Lightly dust the patty with flour and wrap in plastic wrap; refrigerate at least 1 hour, preferably overnight. (The dough will last up to one week refrigerated.) On a lightly floured surface roll out the dough to a thickness of ⅛ to ¼ inch. Very lightly flour top of the dough and fold it into quarters. Carefully place the dough in a

greased and floured 8-inch round *cake* pan (1½ inches deep) so that the corner of the folded dough is centered in the pan. Unfold the dough and arrange it to fit the sides and bottom of pan; press firmly in place. Trim edges. Refrigerate 15 minutes.

2. To prepare the *SWEET-POTATO FILLING*, combine all the ingredients in a mixing bowl. Beat on medium speed of electric mixer until the batter is smooth, about 2 to 3 minutes. Do not overbeat. Set aside.

3. To prepare the *PECAN PIE SYRUP*, combine all the ingredients except the pecans in a mixing bowl. Mix thoroughly on slow speed of electric mixer until the syrup is opaque, about 1 minute; stir in pecans and set aside.

4. To assemble, spoon the sweet-potato filling evenly into the dough-lined cake pan. Pour the pecan syrup on top. Bake in a 325° oven until a knife inserted in the center comes out clean, about 1¾ hours. (**Note**: The pecans will rise to the top of the pie during baking.) Cool and serve with *CHANTILLY CREAM*. Store pie at room temperature for the first 24 hours, then (in the unlikely event there is any left) refrigerate.

Copyright © 1984 by Paul Prudhomme

CHANTILLY CREAM

⅔ cup heavy cream
1 teaspoon vanilla extract
1 teaspoon brandy
1 teaspoon Grand Marnier

¼ cup sugar
2 tablespoons dairy
  sour cream

1. Refrigerate a medium-size bowl and beaters until very cold. Combine cream, vanilla, brandy and Grand Marnier in the bowl and beat with electric mixer on medium speed 1 minute.

2. Add the sugar and sour cream and beat on medium speed just until soft peaks form, about 3 minutes. Do not overbeat.

Makes 2 cups.

Overbeating will make the cream grainy, which is the first step leading to butter. Once grainy you can't return it to its former consistency, but if this ever happens, enjoy it on toast!

Copyright © 1984 by Paul Prudhomme

CAJUN MARTINIS

1 *cayenne or jalapeño pepper*
1 *fifth of gin or vodka*
  Vermouth

Pickled green tomatoes,
okra or eggplant
(optional)

1. Slice the pepper lengthwise without cutting through the stem. Place the pepper in the bottle of gin or vodka. Fill any remaining air space with the vermouth. Recap and refrigerate at least 8 hours and no more than 16. Remove the pepper and store the martinis in the refrigerator until ready to serve.

2. To serve, fill a jar or pitcher with ice and pour gin or vodka over it; strain into serving glasses. Garnish with pickled vegetables if desired.

Be sure to use a bottle of gin or vodka that has never been opened.
Makes a fifth of martinis.

Chef Paul operates Ouber Sprudel, Inc., a USDA approved plant in Melville, Louisiana, which produces hot and regular andouille (smoked sausage) and tasso (cajun ham).

Copyright © 1984 by Paul Prudhomme

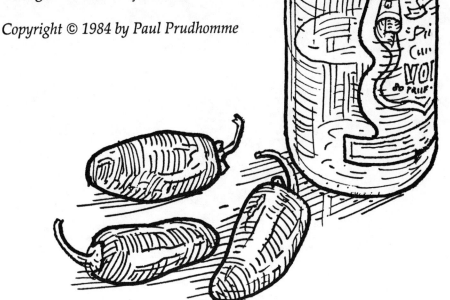

LA PROVENCE

SERVICE · CUISINE

PAR EXCELLENCE

Dinner for Four

Pâté à la Cuillere

Crevette aux Fines Herbes Phyllis Dennery

Salade Tiede d'Écrevisses

Saddle of Rabbit au Poivres Vert

Ragout d'Artichauts

Diplomat Pudding with Sauce Anglaise

Wines:

Freemark Abbey Chardonnay, 1981

Chateau le Gardine Rhone, 1981

Chris Kerageorgiou, Patron et Cuisinier

131

LA PROVENCE

Chris Kerageorgiou, chef extraordinaire: for over a decade his La Provence restaurant has been ranked among New Orleans' ten best in virtually every listing. His L'École de La Provence cooking school has earned him still more honors. His work has been recognized for years with highest praise by the *Mobil Travel Guide, Travel Holiday Magazine*, and innumerable other publications. More than twenty major cookbooks bear his contributions. The television program *Great Chefs of New Orleans* has featured him in both of its series, as have programs as far away as Seattle, Washington. His charitable work and cooking demonstrations on behalf of St. Michael's Children's Home and La Fête are yet another characteristic of this marvelous individual. Chris is a gifted, hard working man with a heart as big as his talent. He understands that it takes work to get to the top. His story is a slice right out of the American dream.

Chris was born Constantin Kerageorgiou on December 7, 1927, in Port Saint Louis, Provence, France. He came to America in 1947 with a drive to absorb as much learning in the restaurant world as he could.

His early training was as a baker, but a desire for broader and newer experiences led him through tutelage as a cook, a waiter, and a maître d'.

He had heard in France the old story about America as the land of opportunity, and even today no one can convince him otherwise. Chris says, "I had this idea at the back of my mind to use my background and accumulate knowledge to someday open a truly fine French restaurant. I wanted it to be out in the country, to be reminiscent of the great houses near my home in Provence, and to be named La Provence." For twenty-five years his life was directed toward that goal.

Finally, in 1972, he crossed Lake Pontchartrain, looking for a place. On September 26, 1972, La Provence celebrated its opening day as a reality and its twenty-fifth anniversary as a dream.

Chris wanted to bring the feeling, not just the cooking, of the French countryside to his house. Those who visit there are sharing a total dining experience, perfected anew each day. The restless spirit which led to the existence of La Provence is now manifested in an ongoing process of creativity which sparkles with innovation and glows with a warmth that can only spring from love.

Highway 190
Lacombe

PÂTÉ À LA CUILLERE
(A simple mousse of duck or chicken liver)

2 pounds duck or chicken
 livers
2 whole eggs
2 ounces cognac
¼ cup Madeira

Salt and pepper, to taste
Pinch of sugar
5 sticks butter
 (room temperature)
Buttered parchment paper

1. In a food processor, purée finely the livers, eggs, cognac, Madeira, salt, pepper, and a pinch of sugar, turning the machine on and off so you won't overheat the ingredients. If the mixture should warm, add a little bit of ice. After all other ingredients are puréed, incorporate the butter in the same manner so as not to overheat.

2. Line a suitable terrine with buttered parchment paper and fill with the puréed ingredients. Place the terrine in a water bath, and bake approximately 30 minutes at 375°.

Slice and serve with toast points or crackers.

CREVETTE AUX FINES HERBES PHYLLIS DENNERY
(Shrimp with fine herbs)
In Honor of Phyllis Dennery

24 shrimp
   Salt and pepper, to taste
2-3 tablespoons olive oil
2-3 shallots, finely chopped
1 clove garlic, finely
   chopped

1 teaspoon of each: basil,
   thyme, chives, parsley,
   tarragon, rosemary
2 tomatoes, peeled,
   deseeded, and diced
¼ cup white wine
½ cup heavy cream

1. Peel and devein the shrimp. Salt and pepper to taste.

2. Place the shrimp in a hot skillet with a little olive oil and the chopped shallots and garlic. Sauté for 1 minute over high heat. Add the herbs and sauté for a few more seconds. Remove the shrimp from the pan, place the tomatoes in the pan, and lightly sauté. Add the wine and cream. Cook about 2 minutes. Check the seasoning. Return the shrimp to the pan for about 1 minute. Remove and serve.

I was thrilled to have Chris create a dish honoring me for my work with the New Orleans Food Festival, La Fête.

SALADE TIEDE D'ÉCREVISSES
(Hot Crawfish Salad)

1 *pound live crawfish*	1 *lettuce (Boston or*
4 *tablespoons oil*	*romaine)*
Shallots, or white or green	2 *tablespoons sherry wine*
onion, chopped	*vinegar*
Fresh tarragon or fresh	*Salt and pepper*
basil	

1. Boil the crawfish without seasoning for approximately 2 minutes. Quick chill, peel, and devein.
2. In a medium skillet, place the oil and shallots. Sauté a few seconds (do not overcook).
3. Add the crawfish and tarragon or basil. Cook for approximately 1 minute.
4. On four separate plates, arrange the lettuce. (You can mix the lettuce, if you like.) Arrange the crawfish on top of the lettuce. Sprinkle with sherry vinegar, pour hot oil and shallots over the crawfish and serve. Salt and pepper to taste.

This is a most unusual appetizer.

SADDLE OF RABBIT AU POIVRES VERT

4 *saddles of rabbit*
2 *pounds pork sausage*
   (not hot)
4 *slices slab bacon*
2 *teaspoons clarified butter,*
   or oil
   Salt and pepper, to taste

¼ *cup brandy*
   Fresh green peppercorns,
   to taste
½ *stick, plus 2 teaspoons*
   cold, unsalted butter
1 *cup dry white wine*

1. Debone each rabbit, remove the saddle, and leave the belly on the saddle. Stuff with sausage. Wrap the slab bacon around the middle, lengthwise.

2. Using string, lace securely the length of the saddles. Preheat the oven to 400°.

3. Sauté on each side in 2 teaspoons butter or oil, until lightly brown. Salt and pepper to taste. Place the rabbit in the preheated oven and cook for 7 minutes.

4. To make the sauce, skim off all grease from the pan used to sauté the rabbit. Deglaze the pan with the brandy. Add the green peppercorns, ½ stick of cold butter, and the wine. Heat over a low flame.

5. Remove the rabbit from the oven, cover with aluminum foil, and let settle for 10 minutes. Slice the saddles at an angle, arrange on a platter, pour the sauce around the meat, and serve.

If you know a hunter who will share his bag of the day, you are assured of fresh rabbit; his reward would be to share the meal. If cooking time is of the essence, use domestic rabbit.

RAGOUT D'ARTICHAUTS
(Fricassee of California artichoke)

6 artichokes	4 cloves garlic, minced
2 lemons	2 cups chicken stock
1 quart cold water	3 tomatoes, seeded and diced
6 strips of bacon, sliced	1 bay leaf
1 medium onion, sliced	

1. To prepare the artichokes, cut off the stems. Pull off outer leaves and cut off one-third of the top. Remove the light inner leaves and the choke. Cut, like a pie, into 6 pieces.

2. Squeeze the juice of the lemons into a pan containing the water. Place the pulp and peel of the lemons into the pan. Place the artichokes into the pan and leave for 5 minutes. Remove and pat dry.

3. In a heavy pan, sauté the bacon, onion, and artichokes until the onion is translucent. Add the garlic and cook 2 minutes longer. Stir in the chicken stock, tomatoes, and the bay leaf. Cook for approximately 15 minutes, until the artichokes are al dente. Remove the bay leaf before serving.

If too much liquid remains, remove the artichokes and reduce until slightly thickened. This recipe will serve 4-6 people, depending on the size of the artichokes, and can be presented as a cold or hot dish.

Be certain to seed the tomatoes. Cut off the tops and squeeze.

DIPLOMAT PUDDING

Raisins
Pound cake
½ cup plus 2 tablespoons
  sugar
4 whole eggs

1 teaspoon vanilla extract
2 cups milk
SAUCE ANGLAISE
Red cherry, for garnish

1. In custard cups, place 6 or 7 raisins on the bottom. Cube the pound cake in small cubes and place with the raisins.

2. In a separate bowl, place the sugar, eggs, and vanilla; mix well. In a pot, bring the milk to a boil; add the milk to the sugar and egg mixture. Blend well. Fill custard cups approximately one-half full, let settle, then finish filling to the top. Bake at 375°, 35 to 40 minutes in a water bath. Test with a cake tester. Cool before refrigerating.

3. To serve, remove the custard from the cup. Place upside down on a plate. Pour *SAUCE ANGLAISE* around the custard and serve. Garnish with a small piece of red cherry.

SAUCE ANGLAISE

2 cups milk   ½ pound sugar
8 egg yolks   1 teaspoon almond extract

1. Bring the milk to a boil in a heavy saucepan.
2. In a mixing bowl, beat the egg yolks, sugar, and almond extract together with a wire whisk until pale in color and the mixture forms a ribbon when the whisk is lifted.
3. Add the hot milk to the mixture slowly, stirring with a spatula. Return the mixture to the pot. Let it simmer for 2 minutes, but do not let it boil. Continue to stir with a spatula. The sauce is ready when it covers the spatula. Remove the pot from the fire and return the mixture to a bowl. Place the bowl in a larger bowl full of ice cubes to cool. Continue to stir with a spatula.

This sauce will hold in the refrigerator for about three days and may be used with cake or fruit.

Dinner for Six

Agnolotti-Alla-Fraccaro
(Crabmeat Ravioli)

Scampi Genovese

Italian Salad with Italian Dressing

Veal Piccata

Rum Maraschino Cream Cake

Cappucino: Italian Style

Wines:

Est.Est.Est

Orvietta

Goffredo Fraccaro, Proprietor and Chef

LA RIVIERA

Those fortunate enough to have cruised the oceans on the famous Italian Line ships such as the Christopher Columbus and the Leonardo DaVinci well remember the exquisite culinary delights served aboard those famous liners.

Goffredo Fraccaro, proprietor/chef of Ristorante La Riviera, was one of those responsible for the gourmet meals aboard ship. By happy chance, one of those ships made port in New Orleans, and Chef Goffredo fell in love with the city. "One day," he said, "I will return to New Orleans to make my home and open a restaurant with my Genovese northern Italian recipes." Sixteen years ago Fraccaro was able to carry out his plan, and now La Riviera is one of the fine restaurants in the suburbs of New Orleans.

Chef Goffredo is not only a culinary master who has received major awards and recognition including a Gold Medal in the 1980 San Francisco Crab Olympics, a Knighthood of the Italian Republic, the Holiday and Mobil three-star awards, and four-star recognition from local food critics. He also possesses a green thumb, as will be seen by the magnificent roses, a bloom on each and every branch, which make up the garden surrounding the entrance to the plantation-style building in which the restaurant is housed.

Elsewhere in this book you will read about Chef Kerageorgio of La Provence. The two chefs—great friends—team up to give cooking demonstrations for charities, conventions, festivals, and cooking schools. Their performances are magnificent and hilarious—one Dallas conventioneer tabbed them as the "Abbot and Costello of the kitchen."

La Riviera, tastefully decorated with paintings, presents a full northern Italian menu with all fresh ingredients. The pasta machines and the special refrigerator holding trays filled with every type of pasta are worth a visit to the kitchen. Chef Goffredo is careful to keep all desserts in a special glass refrigerated case which not only keeps the kitchen flavors and aromas away from the delicate goodies, but also shows them off to perfection.

La Riviera serves the finest of Italian wines to complement the food. The Ristorante is a glorious example of combining warm hospitality with an excellent menu offering a wide choice of tasty foods.

4506 Shores Drive
Metairie

AGNOLOTTI-ALLA-FRACCARO
(Crabmeat Ravioli)

4 cups all-purpose flour	STUFFING
2 eggs	SAUCE
1 cup water	THICK BECHAMEL
1 pinch of salt	Parmesan cheese

1. Put the flour on a large pastry board. Make a well in the middle and add the eggs, water, and salt. Work the eggs and water into the flour, then knead to a smooth elastic dough for about 10 minutes.

2. Roll the dough out as thinly as possible into two sheets. On one sheet arrange teaspoons of the STUFFING in little heaps at regular intervals, 1½ inches apart.

3. Cover with the second sheet of dough and press with the finger around the heaps of stuffing. Cut the agnolotti square with a pastry wheel and make quite sure the edges are firmly sealed.

4. Sprinkle lightly with flour and let them rest for 30 minutes, turning them after 15 minutes.

5. Bring a large pan of salted water to boil, add the agnolotti and cook for 12 minutes. Lift out with a perforated spoon and transfer to a heated serving dish.

6. Cover the Ravioli with the SAUCE. Pour the THICK BÉCHAMEL over the SAUCE and sprinkle with Parmesan cheese.

STUFFING

½ cup chopped green onion	2 tablespoons parsley
1 tablespoon butter	1 pound crab meat, picked
1 egg white	over
	4 tablespoons cracker crumbs

1. Sauté the green onion in the butter and then cool.

2. Add the egg white, parsley, crab, and crumbs to the sautéed green onion.

SAUCE

1 cup whipping cream	Salt, red and white
½ stick butter	pepper, to taste

1. Reduce the cream by one-half.
2. Stir in the butter and seasonings.

THICK BÉCHAMEL

½ cup milk	Pinch of white and red
1 tablespoon butter	pepper
1 tablespoon flour	1 egg yolk
¼ teaspoon salt	

Cook together for 4-5 minutes over low heat all ingredients and then let cool.

SCAMPI GENOVESE

2 pounds raw shrimp	¼ cup chopped parsley
½ cup butter	3 tablespoons lemon juice
1 tablespoon salt	1 tablespoon paprika
6 cloves garlic	6 lemon wedges

1. Preheat the oven to 400°.
2. Remove the shells from the shrimp, leaving the shell on the tail only. Devein and wash under water. Drain on paper towels.
3. Melt the butter in a baking dish in the oven. Then add the salt, garlic, and parsley and mix well.

4. Arrange the shrimp in a single layer in a separate baking dish. Bake uncovered for 5 minutes. Turn the shrimp, sprinkle with lemon juice and paprika. Bake 8 to 10 minutes until tender. (Do not overcook). Arrange the shrimp on a heated serving platter. Pour garlic butter over all. Garnish with lemon wedges.

French bread is a necessity to soak up the sauce.

ITALIAN SALAD WITH ITALIAN DRESSING

Romaine	*6 tomato wedges, for*
Iceberg lettuce	*garnish*
Escarole	*6 anchovies, for garnish*
Endive	*ITALIAN DRESSING*
Garlic	
Chopped olives, for	
garnish	

1. Clean and break all greens with the hands. Mix together. Add some freshly chopped garlic and let chill.
2. Top each salad with chopped olives, a wedge of tomato, and an anchovy. Serve with *ITALIAN DRESSING*

ITALIAN DRESSING

	Crushed red pepper
Olive oil (3 parts)	*(Italian)*
Wine vinegar (1 part)	*Parsley*
Garlic	*Romano cheese*
Oregano	

Blend all together well.

VEAL PICCATA

12 pieces veal scallop
   Salt and pepper, to taste
   Flour
6 tablespoons butter
2 tablespoons finely
   chopped parsley, plus
   more for garnish

Juice from 1 lemon
2 tablespoons hot stock
   (such as beef broth)
   Lemon slices, for garnish

1. Take the veal and pound it until it is flat, but not broken. Each piece should be about the size of a human hand once it has been tenderized in this manner. Salt and pepper both sides, then coat lightly with flour, shaking off the excess.

2. Melt 4 tablespoons of the butter in a wide pan, then turn up heat, add the veal, and fry quickly without browning it for about 1 minute. Remove the veal from the pan and pour in water to rinse out the butter and grease. Then put the veal back in and add parsley, lemon juice, 2 tablespoons butter, and stock. Stir well or "shake" with a fork.

3. As soon as the sauce is bubbling and creamy, remove the pan from the heat. Place the veal on a dish and pour the sauce over the top. Garnish with chopped parsley or a lemon slice dipped in parsley. Serve immediately, 2 pieces of veal to each person.

Cook over a medium flame, watching constantly, as veal browns quickly.

RUM MARASCHINO CREAM CAKE

6 eggs
⅔ cup plus 1 tablespoon
   sugar
2½ teaspoons pure vanilla
   extract
1½ cups flour, sifted twice

1 cup Maraschino cherry
   syrup (from cherries)
1 teaspoon almond extract
2 cups heavy cream, whipped
   Maraschino cherries, for
   decoration

1. Combine the eggs, ⅔ cup sugar, and 1½ teaspoons vanilla in a small mixing bowl. Beat over hot water for 3 to 4 minutes. Remove from the heat and continue to whip for 8 minutes on high speed.
2. Fold in the flour.
3. Pour into a greased and floured 10-inch baking pan.
4. Bake for 35 to 40 minutes at 350°. Cool.
5. Slice the cake into 3 thin layers. Sprinkle with Maraschino cherry syrup flavored with almond extract. Cover each layer with whipped cream flavored with 1 tablespoon sugar and 1 teaspoon vanilla, and decorate the top of the cake with rosettes of whipped cream and whole Maraschino cherries.

CAPPUCINO: ITALIAN STYLE

FOR EACH SERVING:
¼ cup espresso coffee
2 tablespoons steamed milk

Whipped cream
Cinnamon

1. Mix and steam the coffee and milk.
2. Top with whipped cream and dust with cinnamon.

Dinner for Six

Olive Pâté

Oysters Belle Rive

Duck Soup

Avocado with Hearts of Palm

Crabmeat St. Francis

Crêpes à LeRuth

Fresh Lemon Tartelettes

Creole Corn Muffins

Wines:

With the Pâté and the Crab—Montagny, Louis Latour, 1982

With the Oysters—Chalone Pinot Blanc Noir Reserve

With the Duck Soup—Carmenet Sauvignon Blanc

With the Crêpes—Chateau Coutet, 1971

Lee and Larry LeRuth, Owners and Chefs

LE RUTH

Lee and Larry, sons of Warren LeRuth, have now taken over this highly rated restaurant housed in a small grey cottage in Gretna—across the Mississippi River from downtown New Orleans. The decor is turn-of-the-century elegance in a homelike atmosphere, featuring walls hung with a collection of original art and prints. The goal of the two young chefs is to achieve on their own all the awards presented to their father—including a description by *The New York Times* that the restaurant is flawless and superb. Warren is the consultant to his sons, so they should have little difficulty maintaining the high level of excellence at LeRuth's.

Lee was eight years old when he started cooking in the restaurant, and he has been cooking ever since, except for the time spent traveling in Europe, where he became a well-educated oenophile. The restaurant boasts an extensive wine cellar. Lee says, "Ladies put love into cooking, while I put extra flavor into the pots."

LeRuth's menu and presentation are excellent, but don't expect nouvelle—there is none. They serve only classical French cuisine in the Creole manner, influenced by the family's Belgian and Italian heritage. Fresh bread is made daily and the restaurant produces its own vanilla extract and rich ice cream.

When one asks Lee to recommend seasoning, he says, "red pepper for heat, black pepper for aroma, and white pepper for flavor." Larry adds that they are particularly proud of their blonde roux and insists that "what's on the plate must be perfect."

From generation to generation, LeRuth's continues to have a great future in store for gourmets and gourmands as it serves fine food in a truly New Orleans style.

636 Franklin Street
Gretna

OLIVE PÂTÉ

18 round slices of French
    bread, ½" thick
 1 small can pâté de foie
    Strasbourg
½ pound butter, room
    temperature

¼ teaspoon white pepper
½ jigger brandy
½ cup black olives,
    finely chopped

1. Make the French bread croutons by toasting the round slices of bread in the oven until golden.

2. In a mixer, whip the pâté, butter, white pepper, and brandy until completely blended and smooth.

3. By hand, fold the black olives into this mixture until distributed evenly.

4. Allow flavors to set overnight.

5. To serve, scoop the pâté with a small ice cream scoop, 3 scoops per person on a small plate. Serve along with 3 croutons for each person.

Pâté de foie Strasbourg is available in gourmet shops.

This is delicious as an hors d'oeuvre.

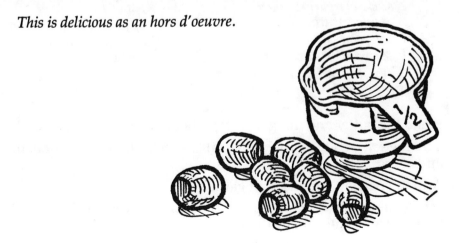

OYSTERS BELLE RIVE

GARLIC BUTTER
VIENNE SAUCE
ARTICHOKE SAUCE

3 *dozen oysters, shucked*
(6 *per person*)

1. Preheat the oven to 400°.
2. Reheat the *GARLIC BUTTER, VIENNE SAUCE,* and *ARTICHOKE SAUCE.*
3. Per person, place 2 oysters each in the bottoms of 3 small ramekins.
4. Fill one ramekin to the top with *GARLIC BUTTER*, one with *VIENNE SAUCE*, and one with *ARTICHOKE SAUCE.*
5. Bake the ramekins for 10 minutes at 400°. Serve immediately.

This recipe takes a little longer, but it's a party dish.

GARLIC BUTTER

2 *sticks butter, room
    temperature*
2 *sticks margarine, room
    temperature*
1 *teaspoon salt*
1 *teaspoon white pepper*
¼ *cup olive oil*

2 *tablespoons white wine*
2 *tablespoons chopped
    parsley*
¼ *cup finely chopped onion*
5 *cloves garlic, finely
    chopped*

1. Blend the butter and margarine together in a mixer, until smooth.
2. Add the salt, white pepper, olive oil, and wine to the butter mixture and blend.
3. Add the parsley, onions, and garlic.
4. Mix on high speed, scraping down the sides occasionally, until the butter turns white, about 10 minutes.
5. Refrigerate until final assembly.

LE RUTH

VIENNE SAUCE

2 cups cream
½ bunch green onions,
   chopped
2 large mushrooms, sliced
1 stick butter

¼ teaspoon salt
⅛ teaspoon white pepper
⅛ teaspoon cayenne pepper
2 tablespoons white wine
1 egg yolk

1. On medium-low heat, reduce the cream by one-third.

2. In a separate pan, sauté the green onions and mushrooms in butter. Season with salt, white pepper, and cayenne pepper. Cook the mixture for 10 minutes over high heat, stirring regularly.

3. Add the white wine and reduced cream. Bring to a boil. Remove from the heat and allow to cool briefly.

4. Whisk in the yolk and bring back to a boil, stirring constantly. Remove from the heat and refrigerate until final assembly.

ARTICHOKE SAUCE

1 cup water
¼ cup olive oil
2 bay leaves
¼ tablespoon thyme
¼ tablespoon salt
⅛ teaspoon white pepper
⅛ teaspoon black pepper

⅛ teaspoon cayenne pepper
10 artichoke hearts, sliced
2 cloves garlic, finely
   chopped
½ cup breadcrumbs
½ cup Romano cheese

1. Place the water, olive oil, and seasonings in a large saucepan. Add the artichokes and garlic and bring to a rolling boil.

2. Stir in the breadcrumbs and cheese and heat thoroughly.

3. Reserve until the final assembly.

DUCK SOUP

2 ducks
1 tablespoon salt
1 tablespoon black pepper
1¾ quarts DUCK STOCK
1 carrot, julienned (matchstick cut)
1 onion, chopped fine
2 ribs celery, chopped fine
3 green onions, chopped
  fine

¾ cup white wine
⅓ cup cornstarch
  Toasted duck skin,
  crumbled
3 tablespoons chopped
  parsley
  Duck meat, julienned
  (matchstick cut)

1. Preheat the oven to 400°

2. Season the ducks with salt and pepper, inside and out. Roast in a pan in the oven for ½ hour. Remove and drain the fat. Lower the oven temperature to 250° and continue to roast for 2 hours. Remove from the oven and allow the ducks to cool enough to handle. Debone, remove all skin and meat, and reserve. Save everything.

3. In a large pot, heat the *DUCK STOCK* to a boil. Add the carrots, onion, celery, and green onions. Simmer until all vegetables are tender.

4. In a separate bowl, combine the wine and cornstarch together. Add this to the soup and stir well. Bring the soup up to a second boil, then reduce the heat and simmer until it thickens slightly.

5. Meanwhile, in a hot oven, bake the duck skins (spread out) on a baking sheet until they are dry to the touch. Remove from the oven and crumble like "bacon bits."

6. Julienne the reserved duck meat.

7. When the soup has simmered about 20 minutes, garnish with chopped parsley, crumbled duck skin, and julienned duck meat.

LE RUTH

DUCK STOCK

2 whole duck carcasses
3 cloves garlic, roughly chopped
½ onion, roughly chopped
1 sprig fresh thyme (or ¼ teaspoon dry thyme)

1¾ quarts water
2 teaspoons salt
¼ teaspoon black pepper
½ teaspoon white pepper
3 bay leaves
3 tablespoons tomato paste

1. Combine all ingredients.
2. Bring up to a boil, reduce to simmer, and cook 1 hour.
3. Strain through a fine strainer. Reserve the stock.

AVOCADO WITH HEARTS OF PALM

3 ripe avocados
2 cups hearts of palm, sliced lengthwise, bias cut
1 head lettuce, washed and torn
2 teaspoons salt
1 teaspoon white pepper
1 teaspoon oregano
2 cloves garlic, finely chopped

2 sprigs fresh thyme (or ½ teaspoon dry thyme)
1⅓ cups olive oil
2 tablespoons red wine vinegar
2 tablespoons white wine vinegar
1 tablespoon parsley, chopped fine

1. Slice the avocado in half, lengthwise. Remove the seed. Fill with hearts of palm, and place on a bed of crisp greens.
2. In a shaker bottle, combine the rest of the ingredients and shake very well. Serve over the chilled salad.

You may mix the greens—romaine, escarole, Boston lettuce, curly endive, etc., for a nicer touch.

An easy, simple, and elegant salad to prepare.

CRABMEAT ST. FRANCIS

3 tablespoons butter
1 small green onion,
 finely chopped
1 large clove garlic,
 finely chopped
⅜ cup onions, finely chopped
⅜ cup celery hearts,
 finely chopped
1 sprig fresh thyme
 (or ¼ teaspoon dry)
½ teaspoon salt
 Pinch of celery seed
⅛ teaspoon red pepper
⅛ teaspoon white pepper
⅛ teaspoon black pepper

2 bay leaves
⅜ cup flour
1 pint cream, gently boiling
1 cup CRAB STOCK,
 gently boiling
⅛ cup white wine, Chalone
 preferred
1 tablespoon chopped parsley
2 egg yolks
1 drop eggshade or yellow
 food color (optional)
1 pound Louisiana "jumbo"
 lump crabmeat,
 picked over
6 coquille shells or
 casserole dishes

1. In a deep rondeau or sauté pan, heat the butter.

2. Add the green onion, garlic, onion, celery heart, and all spices. Sauté well, until vegetables are translucent.

3. Stir in the flour and make a vegetable roux, stirring continuously. Allow to cook over low heat for at least 5 minutes.

4. Add the boiling cream, CRAB STOCK, and wine. Bring up to a boil. Reduce and simmer 15 minutes, then add the parsley.

5. On low heat, stir in the yolks. The soup cannot be reboiled after the yolks have been added. Yellow food color may be added if desired. Remove from direct heat and stir well. Hold warm.

6. Preheat the oven to 400°.

7. Divide the crabmeat onto six coquille shells or small casserole dishes. Cover with approximately ½ cup of sauce and bake at 400°, until bubbly and browned, about 12-15 minutes.

8. Serve immediately and enjoy the goodness of life.

This is a treasured recipe from LeRuth's. It is named for St. Francis, the patron saint of lost people, and of W.F., Lee, and Larry LeRuth.

LE RUTH

CRAB STOCK

3 crabs (fresh, live,
    cracked)
1 pint water
1 bay leaf
1 clove garlic, crushed

⅛ teaspoon thyme
   Juice of ¼ lemon
¼ teaspoon red pepper
½ rib celery

1. In a saucepan, combine all ingredients.
2. Bring up to a boil, then reduce to a simmer.
3. Simmer 45 minutes, or until volume is reduced to 1 cup.
4. Strain and hold refrigerated until needed for sauce.

CRÊPES à LeRUTH

CRÊPES
FILLING

Powdered sugar,
   for garnish
RASPBERRY SAUCE

1. Preheat the oven to 400°.
2. Fill the center of each CRÊPE with a spoonful of FILLING mixture and then fold each crepe over, in half.
3. Place the crepes on a buttered baking sheet and bake at 400° for approximately 15 minutes. Because of the egg whites, the crepes will "souffle" in volume.
4. Sprinkle powdered sugar over the finished crepes.
5. Pour the RASPBERRY SAUCE onto the individual plates and spread evenly to the edges. Place 1 crêpe on this pool of sauce and serve.

LE RUTH

CRÊPES

1 *whole egg*	¼ *teaspoon salt*
½ *cup milk*	½ *teaspoon sugar*
⅓ *cup flour*	*Oil, to grease crêpe pans*

1. Mix all ingredients in a bowl and whip until well-blended.
2. Preheat the crêpe pan, grease very well, and carefully add in 1 spoonful of the batter.
3. Distribute this batter evenly in the pan and cook until the edges turn slightly brown.
4. With a spatula or palette knife, flip the crêpe and cook until done.
5. Repeat until all the batter is used. Crêpes may be stacked, if made in advance.

RASPBERRY SAUCE

1 *pint fresh or frozen raspberries*	¼ *cup water*
	¼ *cup sugar*

1. Purée the raspberries.
2. Combine in a saucepan over low heat the raspberry purée, water, and sugar.
3. Reduce until thickened. Reserve.

LE RUTH

FILLING

2 lemons, skin (rind)
  and juice
½ cup water
½ cup sugar

2 tablespoons flour
2 eggs, separated
½ tablespoon butter, room
  temperature

1. Grate the skin off the lemon lightly with the small size holes of a cheese grater, trying not to remove any of the bitter white parts.

2. Squeeze the juice from the lemons; strain the seeds out.

3. In a saucepan, boil the lemon juice and skin, the water, and the sugar.

4. In a separate bowl, beat the flour and the egg yolks together well. Stir this mixture into the boiling lemon base and stir continuously. Cook the mixture until it thickens. Add in the butter and stir well to incorporate.

5. In a separate, clean bowl (may wipe out with lemon juice or vinegar to be certain it is oil and fat free), beat the whites until they are fluffy and hold soft peaks.

6. Fold ¼ cup of the lemon base into the whites.

FRESH LEMON TARTELETTES

4 *tablespoons sugar*
1 *stick butter, room*
    temperature
1 *stick margarine, room*
    temperature

1 *egg yolk*
1¾ *cups flour*
⅛ *teaspoon salt*
1 *tablespoon water*
    FILLING

1. Cream the sugar, butter, and margarine with a mixer. Add the egg yolk. Blend well. Add the flour and salt. Blend until this mixture comes together. Add the water. Blend in well. Allow to refrigerate 4 hours (to rest the dough, so it will soften and not be tough).

2. Preheat the oven to 400°.

3. Line 18 small, round tartelette pans (each about 2½ inches wide) with the crust. This will give you 3 per person. Fill the tartelettes with the *FILLING* and bake until crisp, approximately 45 minutes.

4. Cool, remove from the pans, and serve.

FILLING

2 *lemons, skin (rind) and*
    juice
3 *whole eggs*

¾ *cup sugar*
2 *tablespoons butter*

1. Grate the skin off the lemon lightly with the small size holes of a cheese grater, trying not to remove any of the bitter white part.

2. Squeeze the juice from the lemons; strain the seeds out.

3. Combine all the ingredients. Blend well.

CREOLE CORN MUFFINS

1 stick butter, room temperature	¼ teaspoon cayenne pepper
1¼ cups corn flour	2 whole eggs
1¼ cups all-purpose flour	⅝ pint milk
2 tablespoons baking powder	⅛ cup cooking oil
½ tablespoon salt	½ bunch green onions, chopped fine

1. Preheat the oven to 325°.
2. Grease the muffin pan very heavily with the room temperature butter.
3. In a large bowl, combine all remaining ingredients and blend well.
4. Distribute this batter into the muffin pan evenly; there may be a little extra to partially fill a second pan.
5. Bake at 325° for about 20 minutes, or until golden brown.
6. Remove from the muffin pans and serve fresh and hot, with butter.

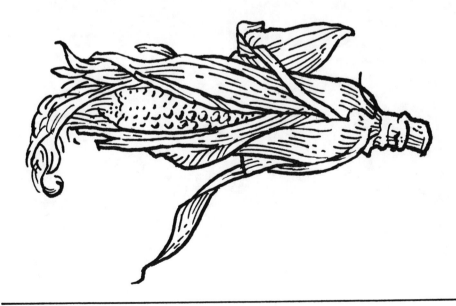

Dinner for Four

Oysters Maras

Solari's Market Salad with Italian Dressing

*Hickory Grilled Shrimp and Andouille Brochettes with
Creole Mustard Sauce*

Mr. B's Chocolate Cake

Wines:

With the Oysters and Salad—Vichon Chevier Blanc, 1982

With the Shrimp—Trelethen Chardonnay, 1982

With the Cake—Piper Sonoma, Brut, 1981

Ralph and Cindy Brennan, Proprietors

Gerard Maras, Executive Chef

Jimmy Smith, Creole Chef

MR. B'S

Mr. B's, a bistro type restaurant, operated by two third generation restaurateurs, Cindy and Ralph Brennan, sister and brother, members of the family which operates Commander's Palace, has continued its proprietors' reputation as purveyors of fine New Orleans food and is attracting many of our younger gourmets.

The restaurant is located at the corner of Royal and Iberville Streets, in the heart of the famous French Quarter. To New Orleanians, Royal and Iberville is a corner noted for fine food for almost 100 years. It was the location of Solari's, a revered retail market specializing in and famous for fine meats, fresh fruit, produce, and wines. Solari's featured breakfast and lunch counters where it seemed half of the city ate.

Mr. B's has true bistro charm, with paneled walls, hardwood floors, etched glass, and a jazz pianist. The kitchen is open, and guests may watch the preparation of the restaurant's specialties, which include fresh seafood grilled over an open hickory fire, pasta, and irresistible desserts. A fine American wine cellar and a magnificent bar complete the delights available to the gourmets who patronize this most attractive café.

Mr. B's has a definite New Orleans style combined with a contemporary flair. The restaurant's two chefs, Gerard Maras and Jimmy Smith, complement each other perfectly as they work with classic Creole recipes, spices, and seasonings. The chefs have lightened the sauces, and their cooking techniques produce lighter and more flavorsome dishes. Maras, a New Yorker, is executive chef and is responsible for the flair, while Smith, a Cajun from South Louisiana, makes certain that each dish at Mr. B's has that special New Orleans Creole touch.

Cindy and Ralph Brennan were featured in American Express' *Food and Wine* as exemplifying the new generation in American cuisine.

201 Royal Street

OYSTERS MARAS

4 tablespoons chopped
    shallots
4 cloves garlic, minced
4 tablespoons diced fresh
    tomatoes
4 tablespoons white wine
24 large oysters

½ teaspoon each: seafood
    seasoning, tarragon,
    basil, crushed red pepper,
    and thyme
2 teaspoons Dijon mustard
4 teaspoons chopped green
    onions
10 tablespoons cold butter

1. Place the shallots, garlic, tomatoes, wine, oysters, and seasonings in a sauté pan. Bring to a quick boil and remove the oysters.
2. Add the mustard and green onions. Reduce the liquid by half.
3. Swirl in the cold butter and bring to a boil. Add the oysters and adjust the seasoning. Serve at once.

SOLARI'S MARKET SALAD

Leaf lettuce
Escarole
Romaine
12 Greek olives
12 tomato wedges
16 peeled cucumber
    wedges

8 ounces Gorgonzola cheese
16 thin slices Bermuda
    onions
8 pepperoni slices
    ITALIAN DRESSING

1. Wash, dry, and tear the greens into bite-size pieces.
2. Place the mixed greens on large salad plates. Place 3 Greek olives, 3 tomato wedges, and 4 peeled wedges of cucumber around the greens. Place a 2-ounce slice of Gorgonzola cheese on the lettuce, 3-4 thin slices Bermuda onion over the cheese, and 2 pepperoni slices on each side of the cheese. Lace with ¼ cup *ITALIAN DRESSING* for each salad.

ITALIAN DRESSING

½ teaspoon dry mustard
½ teaspoon water
¾ cup olive oil
½ clove fresh garlic,
   crushed and diced
2 tablespoons finely diced
   onion
½ teaspoon basil

¼ teaspoon thyme
½ teaspoon salt
¼ teaspoon black pepper,
   crushed
1 tablespoon chopped parsley
¼ cup red wine vinegar
1 tablespoon diced pimiento

1. Mix the dry mustard with ½ teaspoon of water in a mixing bowl. Let set 3-4 minutes.
2. Add all the ingredients except the vinegar, oil and pimiento. After mixing, add the vinegar.
3. Whisk in the oil, then add in the pimiento. Adjust the seasoning.

HICKORY GRILLED SHRIMP AND ANDOUILLE BROCHETTES

2 red bell peppers, cut
   in 1" pieces
2 green bell peppers, cut
   in 1" pieces
1 pound andouille sausage,
   sliced on the bias about
   ⅝" thick

16 jumbo shrimp, peeled,
   with tail on
   SEAFOOD SEASONING
   (see page 63)
1 pound butter, melted
   Rice
   CREOLE MUSTARD
   SAUCE

1. Place the peppers, andouille, and shrimp on skewers, alternating in the same pattern, 4 shrimp per person. Season with seafood seasoning and coat with a small amount of melted butter.

2. Cook over a grill, turning and basting with melted butter until the shrimp are cooked through. Serve with rice and *CREOLE MUSTARD SAUCE.*

Andouille is a regional sausage. If not available any good Polish sausage will do.

CREOLE MUSTARD SAUCE

¼ cup white wine
¼ medium onion, diced
1 bay leaf
1 sprig fresh thyme
1¼ cups veal stock*
1¼ cups heavy cream
½ tablespoon roux*

4 tablespoons Creole mustard
1 tablespoon Dijon mustard
4 tablespoons cold butter, cut in small pieces
Salt and pepper, to taste

1. Put the white wine, onion, bay leaf, and thyme in a sauce pot. On the stove, reduce by one-half.
2. Add the veal stock and reduce again by one-half.
3. Add the cream. Bring to a boil. Whip in the roux. Simmer for 5 minutes.
4. Whip in the mustards and simmer for 5 minutes more.
5. Whip in the butter, one piece at a time. Season with salt and pepper to taste. Remove from the heat and strain.

Use your favorite version of veal stock and roux.

MR. B's CHOCOLATE CAKE

1 pound butter
2 cups sugar
2 teaspoons baking powder
2 teaspoons vanilla
4 eggs, lightly whipped
2 cups cake flour
2 cups cocoa powder

1 teaspoon baking soda
2 cups sour cream
   Madeira wine
   Raspberry preserves
   CHOCOLATE MOUSSE
   GANACHE

1. Cream the butter and sugar together. Add the baking powder, vanilla, and eggs to the butter mixture. Scrape the bowl constantly.

2. Sift the cake flour, cocoa powder, and baking soda into a bowl. Add the flour mixture to the other ingredients along with the sour cream. Mix just to incorporate and finish mixing by hand. Do not overmix.

3. Bake in a buttered, dusted cake pan at 350° for 40 minutes. Remove from the oven and cool on a rack. Slice into three sections lengthwise.

4. Sprinkle the cake slices with Madeira wine. Spread a very thin layer of raspberry preserves over each cake layer.

5. Place ¾ of an inch of CHOCOLATE MOUSSE between each layer of cake. There will be three layers of cake and three layers of mousse, one of which will be on the top.

6. With a cake knife, spread a very thin layer of Mousse on the outside of the cake.

7. Chill the assembled cake well, then coat the cake with GANACHE.

Whipped cream would be too much!

CHOCOLATE MOUSSE

6 egg yolks
1½ pounds sweet chocolate,
    melted very slowly
¼ cup water

1 stick butter
2 cups heavy cream,
    sweetened and
    whipped

1. Add the egg yolks to the melted sweet chocolate.
2. Combine the water and butter with the chocolate mixture and allow to cool.
3. Fold in the sweetened, whipped heavy cream.

GANACHE

1½ pounds sweet chocolate,
    melted
1 stick butter, softened
1 cup milk, room temperature

1 cup heavy cream, room
    temperature

1. Melt the sweet chocolate in a double boiler, stirring by hand.
2. Add the butter, milk, and heavy cream until incorporated.

TRATTORIA ROMA

Dinner for Four

Lumache all' Aliata Piccante

Bucatini Matriciana

Involtini di Manzo al Barolo

Zucchini Ripiene

Zabaglione

Espresso

Wines:

Fattoria Paradiso

Albana di Romagna

Vittorio di Marco and Giacomo Rugirello, Proprietors

Vittorio di Marco, Chef

There is a certain part of the French Quarter in old New Orleans where a lot of new things are happening. You'll find Trattoria Roma across the street from the recently opened shopping center located in the buildings known as Jax Brewery. The Restaurant is near the Moon Walk along the Mississippi and the New Orleans Steamboat wharves where the Natchez, the Jean Lafitte, and other stern-wheelers dock. Not far up the road, the Rouse Company is constructing another one of its famous complexes.

The Vieux Carré is a wonderful setting for this small ristorante where Vittorio Di Marco and Giacomo Rugirello operate a jewel which offers nouvelle gourmet Italian cuisine. The two proprietors say, "We cook and serve what's best." The menu lists innumerable types of pasta, veal, prosciutto, escargot*, and chicken, pounded and prepared in many ways. The joy on Giacomo's face as he helps you choose your menu, the excellent service of your waiter, and the deluxe selection of wine all add up to a delightful evening.

These two men, both from Italy, trained under the brothers De Montes' school in Rome. Vittorio, who was King Farouk's favorite chef at Rome's famous Casina Valadier, was also trained in Brussels, Copenhagen, and London, and finally opened his own restaurant in Chicago. Giacomo, also trained in Europe's capitals, met Vittorio in the Windy City, and the two agreed to come to New Orleans.

The lively proprietors say they came because of the cold in Chicago, but who knows if that's the real reason. New Orleans is fortunate to have Trattoria Roma in place, and all we can do is enjoy its pleasures and hope the restaurant is here for a long time.

Vittorio, who has "nouvellized" his grandmother's cookbook, and Giacomo proudly proclaim that "we will complete the patio, and the second floor will become a lounge."

Go early to the Trattoria to make certain there is enough scampi, and sample at least three of the pastas. You'll be able to catch your breath back via a walk around Jackson Square with a view of the cathedral— just to the left of the front door.

Please excuse our using a French word for an Italian dish written in English.

611 Decatur Street

*LUMACHE ALL'ALIATA PICCANTE

24 snails
1 teaspoon chopped garlic
½ cup olive oil
1 teaspoon cayenne red
   pepper, crushed
2 tablespoons breadcrumbs

Wild fennel, to taste
Salt, to taste
Black pepper, to taste
2 (6-ounce) ladles tomatoes,
   crushed and strained

In a pan, place the snails in a mixture of the garlic, olive oil, cayenne pepper, and breadcrumbs, adding the fennel, salt, and pepper to taste. Sauté for 3 minutes, then add the ladles of tomatoes and continue to sauté for 5 additional minutes. Serve on a hot plate.

*Now it's written in Italian.

BUCATINI MATRICIANA

1 pound thick, long pasta,
   100% Semolina noodles
4 tablespoons olive oil
2 tablespoons natural,
   cured Gunciale (bacon),
   cooked and finely chopped

4 green onions, finely chopped
5 leaves fresh basil
6 (6-ounce) ladles tomatoes
   sammarsano*
4 tablespoons Picorino
   Romano, grated

1. Boil the pasta until it reaches al dente, then strain.
2. Prepare a red sauce by mixing the olive oil, Gunciale, onions, basil, and the tomatoes. Heat thoroughly before serving.
3. Cover each plate with the sauce and place the noodles in the sauce, then sprinkle the grated cheese over the plate. Place additional grated cheese on the table.

*If you don't plan to do your grocery shopping in Rome, be prepared to use Del Verdi brand or other whole peeled tomatoes.

INVOLTINI DI MANZO AL BAROLO

1 teaspoon pine nuts	Flour
1 teaspoon raisins	4 tablespoons butter
4 slices Fontinella cheese	GAROFOLATO SAUCE
4 leaves fresh sage	
4 (1-inch) slices tenderloin of beef	

1. Mix the nuts, raisins, cheese, and sage thoroughly to make a stuffing.
2. Roll the beef over the stuffing and lightly dust with flour.
3. Sauté the beef in the butter.
4. Place the beef in a pot, cover with *GAROFOLATO SAUCE*, cover the pot, and cook 15 minutes at 500°. If the sauce is too runny, reduce over the flame until a firm consistency is reached.

GAROFOLATO SAUCE

1 small white onion	Garlic, to taste
1 small carrot	½ cup consommé
2 stalks celery	½ cup Barolo wine
Pinch of parsley	

1. Grind together the onion, carrot, celery, parsley, and a touch of garlic.
2. Place in a bowl and add the consommé and wine.

ZUCCHINI RIPIENE

4 *zucchini*	1 *cup breadcrumbs*
Salt	½ *cup cooked (al dente)*
Pepper	*rice*
½ *cup olive oil*	2 *eggs*
1 *large white onion,*	4 *teaspoons Parmesan cheese*
finely chopped	*Tomato sauce*

1. Cut each zucchini in half lengthwise and remove (lightly) the seeds. Season with salt and pepper to taste and bake for 5 minutes at 500°. Remove the zucchini and let cool.

2. Place the olive oil, chopped onion and zucchini in a frying pan and fry until a golden color is reached. Stir in the breadcrumbs and rice and let cool for 5 minutes. Add a mixture of the eggs and Parmesan cheese. Place the entire mixture in a pastry bag and squeeze over the zucchini. Cover with plain tomato sauce sprinkled with Parmesan cheese.

Serve hot or cold.

ZABAGLIONE

8 *egg yolks*	*Vanilla ice cream*
8 *tablespoons sugar*	8 *strawberries, chopped*
1¼ *cups Marsala wine*	

1. Place the yolks of the eggs in a steel bowl; add the sugar and the Marsala wine. Place the bowl on top of a pot of boiling water and stir easily—*DO NOT PERMIT THE MIXTURE TO COOK.*

2. When the mixture puffs up, place 1 cup of the mixture over ½ scoop of vanilla ice cream in each of four champagne glasses. Sprinkle chopped strawberries on top.

This is a delicious, light dessert. Serve in stem crystal.

Dinner for Four

Artichoke Mathilda

Squash and Shrimp Bisque

Asparagus and Crabmeat Salad

Trout Lacombe

Almond Tart

Wines:

With the First Three Courses—Robert Mondavi Fumé Blanc

With the Trout—Chateau St. Michel Chardonnay

With the Dessert—Domaine Chandon Champagne

Joann Clevenger and Jason Clevenger, Proprietors

Jason Clevenger, Chef

UPPERLINE

One of the newer restaurants in "uptown" New Orleans materialized because Jason Clevenger—who has now reached the ripe old age of twenty-five—started cooking in his mama Joann's kitchen when he was twelve years old. Joann's father worked in every area in Louisiana where the hunting and fishing were good, so Joann was raised in areas of the state which produced some of the finest products of Louisiana. As a young girl, Joann took a job as a waitress, and she gives full credit to her early jobs as the training ground which gave her an insight into how to deal with the public.

Jason was educated at top schools in New Orleans but continued his "home grown" apprenticeship because he loved to eat—as a matter of fact, he feels that most young chefs haven't eaten enough and follow recipes too mechanically, without knowing what the end product should look and taste like.

Jason, after graduating from high school, got his first job as a bus boy at the Pontchartrain Hotel's Caribbean Room and was "promoted" to working in the storeroom, where in his spare time he did odd jobs for the chef. In this manner, he not only learned about purchasing, but also about preparing food for restaurant meals. While still in his teens, Jason took a job as the third cook at Café Sbisa, where he became head chef just after his twenty-first birthday.

Shortly after this, Joann noticed a "For Rent" sign on a building on Upperline Street which had housed a neighborhood restaurant she had patronized at breakfast every morning in her earlier years. Inquiries led to the knowledge that the owners would sell; thus was born the Upperline, now one of the most popular owner-operated neighborhood restaurants—where the service is only equalled by the food—where special requests are met—where reservations are always honored—where all ingredients including herbs are fresh—where no commercial mixes are used—where there are no strict dress codes—where the guests, who vary from the college crowd to the older gourmet types in New Orleans, as well as visitors to the city, always leave the restaurant with a smile or Joann knows the reason why. In its few short years of operation, the Upperline has received recognition in the local press, and national recognition in *USA Today*, in *Food and Wine*, and in other magazines. Chef Jason says: "Buy the best ingredients possible, cook in a simple manner, season to enhance flavors not to disguise, and taste and taste again."

1413 Upperline Street

ARTICHOKE MATHILDA

4 medium artichokes	½ pound bay scallops
8 quarts plus 3 cups water	HOLLANDAISE SAUCE
1 tablespoon salt	1 lemon, seeded and cut
1 tablespoon olive oil	into quarters, for garnish
½ cup dry white wine	4 sprigs parsley, for garnish
4 black peppercorns	

1. The artichokes must be started at least 1 hour before service and may be prepared up to 6 hours before use.

2. Bring the 8 quarts of water to a boil and add the salt and olive oil. Place the artichokes in the water and cover. Boil for at least 30 minutes. They are done when a leaf comes out easily. Drain and cool. Clean by removing all of the leaves and saving. Discard the choke and scrape the hairy part off the artichoke bottom. Cut the stem off so that the bottom sits level.

3. Put the 3 cups water, white wine, and peppercorns into a medium-size skillet and bring to a light boil. Reduce to a simmer and add the scallops and cooled artichoke bottoms. Poach gently for 1½-2 minutes. Remove the scallops and bottoms.

4. Place 1 bottom on each of four salad plates. Arrange some of the leaves overlapping around the base. Divide the scallops and place in a mound on top of each artichoke. Spoon 2-3 tablespoons of *HOLLANDAISE* over the scallops. Garnish with lemon quarters and parsley.

HOLLANDAISE SAUCE

3 egg yolks
Pinch of salt
Pinch of cayenne pepper

Juice of ½ lemon
1½ cups warm clarified butter

Put the egg yolks in a large, warm metal bowl (not aluminum). Add the salt, pepper, and lemon juice and mix together with a whisk. Continue to whisk and *slowly* add the melted butter. The mixture should thicken.

SQUASH AND SHRIMP BISQUE

1 pound yellow squash, sliced
7 cups water
½ stick butter
⅓ cup white flour
⅓ cup chopped onion
⅓ cup chopped, green bell pepper

¼ teaspoon cayenne pepper
½ teaspoon whole thyme
2 bay leaves
½ teaspoon salt
⅓ pound raw peeled shrimp, chopped
⅓ cup heavy cream

1. Boil the squash in the water until tender, about 25 minutes. Strain the squash, reserving the liquid. Purée the squash.

2. Melt the butter in a 4-quart saucepan and whisk in the flour. Continue to whisk over medium heat until light golden, approximately 6-7 minutes.

3. Add the onions and bell peppers. Sauté the mixture for 5 minutes and then add the puréed squash, reserved squash liquid, cayenne pepper, thyme, bay leaves, and salt. Simmer for 10 minutes.

4. Add the chopped shrimp and heavy cream and simmer for another 30 minutes. Correct the seasoning.

Serve in soup bowls.

ASPARAGUS AND CRABMEAT SALAD

4 quarts water
Salt
1 pound fresh asparagus,
   trimmed
1 head bibb lettuce

½ pound fresh lump
   crabmeat, picked over
8 slices pimiento
DRESSING

1. Bring 4 quarts of salted water to a boil in a large pot. Cook the asparagus until just done; it should still have a little crunch to it. Remove and place in ice water for several minutes.

2. Wash and separate the lettuce leaves.

3. Pick through the crabmeat to remove any shell.

4. Arrange the lettuce on chilled salad plates. Place the asparagus in the middle of the plate and top with crabmeat. Arrange the pimiento in crosses over the crabmeat. Put 2 tablespoons of DRESSING over the crabmeat. Serve with extra DRESSING on the side.

This recipe is lovely on a hot summer evening or for lunch.

DRESSING

1 egg
½ cup red wine vinegar
¼ cup Dijon mustard
2 tablespoons chopped
   shallots
1 teaspoon fresh ground
   pepper

¼ teaspoon salt
1 tablespoon chopped fresh
   basil
1½ cups salad oil

Put all of the dressing ingredients except the salad oil into a food processor. Turn the machine on and slowly pour the oil in through the hopper. When finished, pour the dressing into a suitable container and chill.

TROUT LACOMBE

2 tablespoons butter
½ cup sliced mushrooms
½ cup chopped green onions
½ pound crawfish tails
¼ cup water
¾ cup heavy whipping cream
⅛ plus ¼ teaspoon cayenne
  pepper
⅛ plus ½ teaspoon salt

¼ teaspoon chopped fresh
  dill
½ teaspoon brandy
¼ cup clarified butter or
  cooking oil
1 cup yellow corn flour
1 egg
½ cup milk
4 (6- to 8-ounce) trout fillets

1. Begin the sauce 15 minutes before serving. Heat a medium saucepan and add the 2 tablespoons butter, mushrooms, and green onions. Sauté for 2 minutes. Add the crawfish tails and water and simmer until almost all of the liquid has evaporated. Add the cream, ⅛ teaspoon cayenne pepper, ⅛ teaspoon salt, the dill, and the brandy. Simmer for 5-7 minutes, until thick.

2. While the sauce is cooking, heat a large sauté pan and add the clarified butter. Combine the flour, ½ teaspoon salt, and ¼ teaspoon pepper in one bowl and whisk the egg and milk in another. Dip the trout fillets in the egg wash and then dredge in the flour mixture. Place carefully in the hot skillet. Cook approximately 2 minutes on one side and then turn and cook another 2 minutes. Transfer the fish to serving plates and top with the sauce. Serve immediately.

Small peeled shrimp may be substituted for the crawfish tails.

ALMOND TART

CRUST:
- 1½ cups white flour
- 1½ tablespoons sugar
- ¼ pound plus 1 tablespoon cold butter, cut into slices
- 1½ tablespoons cold water

FILLING:
- 1½ cups whipping cream
- 1½ cups sliced blanched almonds
- 1 cup sugar
- 1½ tablespoons Grand Marnier

1. The CRUST can be made a day in advance. Put the flour and sugar into a food processor. Turn the machine on and feed and butter through the hopper. When the mixture becomes mealy, pour in the cold water. The dough should form into a ball on the top of the blades. Chill the dough for at least 15 minutes. Roll the dough out and linean 8-inch glass pie pan. Bake at 350° for 15 minutes.

2. To make the FILLING, put the cream, almonds, and sugar in a heavy bottomed saucepan and bring the mixture to a boil. Simmer for 15 minutes and add the Grand Marnier. Pour the mixture into the prepared pie shell. Bake at 300° for 40-45 minutes.

Cool and cut into wedges. Serve with whipped cream, if desired.

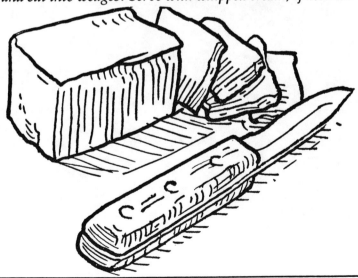

Dinner for Six

Crawfish Versailles

Artichoke Soup au Boursin

Pear Sorbet

Duckling Flamande

Almond Cookies with Mocha Sauce and Hazelnut Cream

Demi Tasse

Wines:

With the Crawfish—Cakebread Sauvignon Blanc, 1983

With the Duckling—Rutherford Hill Merlot, 1981

With the Dessert—Schramsberg-Blanc de Blancs, 1982

Gunter and Evelyn Preuss, Proprietors

Gunter Preuss, Chef

THE VERSAILLES

Gunter Preuss, owner-chef of the Versailles Restaurant, located on famous St. Charles Avenue where guests can see the rolling National Monument Trolley Cars, likes to say, "My establishment is an experience, not an experiment." The restaurant has received six Travel/Holiday awards, and Preuss is the only "Vice Conseilleur de Culinaire" of the Chaines de Rotisseurs—an honor never previously bestowed upon a professional chef in the New Orleans area.

One sees that intimate elegance created during the opulent period of Louis XIV and his Versailles—even to the Sun King Bar, with its separate entrance.

The menu is essentially French but with a decidedly New Orleans flavor, not unusual in New Orleans except that both Gunter and his co-proprietor wife, Evelyn, were born in Berlin. The Preuss training in England, France, Switzerland, Sweden, and Germany has given him the experience which permits Gunter to create dishes beyond the belief of ordinary mortals. Since 1972, when they commenced their direction of the Versailles, it has become one of the few restaurants in New Orleans featuring Boeuf au Moelle, chanterelles, and sweet breads, and during that period it has climbed the culinary ladder to its highest rung.

Business and professional visitors to the city find the Versailles not only an excellent place to dine, but also an excellent location in which to entertain small groups. The restaurant is divided into medium sized dining rooms, permitting private parties not to interfere with the individual diners. Coats are required, which adds to the formality of this quiet, elegant restaurant with superb service, indicative of the close personal supervision of the proprietors.

2100 St. Charles Avenue

CRAWFISH VERSAILLES

1 teaspoon sliced green
   onions
¼ teaspoon minced garlic
1 teaspoon minced dry
   shallots
2 tablespoons butter
½ cup white wine
   Juice of ¼ lemon
1¾ cups medium béchamel
   sauce

1 tablespoon fresh dill
1½ pounds freshly boiled
   crawfish tails
Salt, to taste
Pinch of cayenne pepper
Parmesan cheese
6 boiled crawfish

1. Sauté the onions, garlic, and shallots in butter for 2 minutes without browning.
2. Add the white wine and lemon juice, then reduce by one-half.
3. Add the béchamel sauce and dill and reduce by another one-third.
4. Add the crawfish tails and simmer for 10 minutes. Salt to taste and add a pinch of cayenne pepper.
5. To serve, put in ramekins or small sea shells, sprinkle with freshly grated Parmesan cheese, and bake at 350° until the cheese is golden.

Garnish with a boiled crawfish and serve.

Crabmeat may be substituted for crawfish tails.

ARTICHOKE SOUP AU BOURSIN

1 *small onion, diced*
1 *tablespoon chopped dry*
  shallots
½ *tablespoon chopped garlic*
2 *tablespoons olive oil*
1 *(14-ounce) can artichoke*
  hearts, drained, with
  juice reserved

2 *(14-ounce) cans chicken*
  broth
2 *bay leaves*
  Salt and pepper, to taste
6 *tablespoons Boursin herb*
  cheese (without pepper)

1. Sauté the onions, shallots, and garlic in oil until limp. Add the artichoke juice, chicken broth, and bay leaves. Bring to boil, then simmer for 15 minutes.

2. Add the drained artichokes, simmer for 15 more minutes, and correct the seasoning. Remove the bay leaves.

3. To each cup, add 1 tablespoon of Boursin herb cheese.

Souper!

PEAR SORBET

1 *cup sugar*
2 *cups water*

2 *cups puréed fresh, ripe*
  pears
¼ *cup lemon juice*

1. Make a syrup of sugar and water over low heat.

2. Peel and slice the pears, put them in blender, and add them to syrup immediately to keep them from turning dark. Cool and add the lemon juice. Place in the freezer.

3. Beat the sorbet before it has started to freeze in order to break up ice crystals and beat once again before it has set.

DUCKLING FLAMANDE

3 *(3- to 3½-pound) ducklings*
Salt, pepper, and rosemary
1 *(14-ounce) can Bing*
cherries

6 *pears, poached and peeled*
DUCK SAUCE

1. Season the ducklings with salt, pepper, and rosemary. Roast at 350° for about 2½ hours.
2. Remove the ducklings, split in half with a French knife, and bone.
3. Sauté the Bing cherries and spread over the poached pears. Serve one-half duckling on each plate with *DUCK SAUCE*.

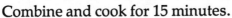

DUCK SAUCE

¼ *cup orange cognac*
¼ *cup port wine*

2 *cups rich brown sauce,*
rich stock, or demi glaze

Combine and cook for 15 minutes.

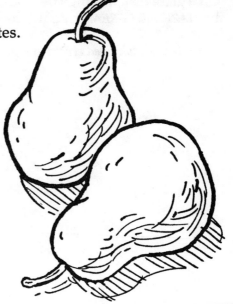

ALMOND COOKIES WITH MOCHA SAUCE AND HAZELNUT CREAM

¼ tablespoon butter	¼ tablespoon almond extract
½ cup sugar	¼ teaspoon vanilla extract
¼ cup egg whites	MOCHA SAUCE
⅓ cup chopped almonds	HAZELNUT CREAM

1. Cream the butter in a bowl with the sugar. Add the egg whites. Mix well with a rubber spatula. Blend the finely chopped almonds, almond extract, and vanilla extract into the butter/sugar mixture.

2. Preheat the oven to 425°. Smear baking sheets with soft butter. Drop 1 tablespoon globs of batter on the sheets, spacing them 3 inches apart. With the back of a spoon, smear out each blob to form a thin 2½-inch dish. Bake for 4 minutes; when done, use a metal spatula under the cookie.

3. Lift each cookie over a small glass dish and form it into a cup. Let them cool off.

4. On a glass dish, arrange the cookie with *MOCHA SAUCE*, then scoop the *HAZELNUT CREAM* into the cookie.

Decorate with whipped cream and glazed cherries if desired.

MOCHA SAUCE

½ pound butter
¼ cup sugar
2 teaspoons Sanka coffee

¼ cup brandy
½ pint whipping cream

1. Melt the butter and add the sugar. Whip until the sugar has dissolved.
2. Dissolve the coffee in the brandy and add to the warm butter mixture. Let cool at room temperature, then add the whipping cream (not whipped) to the mixture. Keep the sauce at room temperature and do not chill.

HAZELNUT CREAM

6 ounces hazelnut paste
¾ cup egg yolk
4 tablespoons sugar
1 tablespoon gelatin

¼ cup brandy
1 cup milk
1 pint whipping cream,
  whipped

1. Add all ingredients except the whipped cream together. Whip in a double boiler until thick.
2. Cool in the refrigerator, then fold in the whipped cream. Cool for 1 hour, then serve.

LAGNIAPPE*

*Lagniappe is the Creole term for something extra.

You can't do justice to our town's food if you just visit restaurants or hotel dining rooms. There are unique eating spots in New Orleans which are top quality. I offer them, mostly for snack time, although there are a few where one can eat a full meal.

New Orleans is filled with many establishments which serve our famous "Red Beans and Rice," particularly on Mondays. *Buster Holmes'* at *Jax Brewery* is a super place to find them.

A Po' Boy sandwich is created on a long loaf of French bread (made with New Orleans' water!) split lengthwise, spread with butter, mustard, mayonnaise, plus lettuce and tomatoes; and the one with the best ham we've ever found is at *Mother's* (401 Poydras Street).

New Orleans is also famous for its coffee houses where you can sit leisurely with your café au lait (with chicory) and dunk your beignets (Creole doughnuts). One spot is the *Café du Monde* in the French Market.

If you are heading for our great Audubon Park Zoo, you may be lucky enough to find a *Manuel's* cart with Hot Tamales on the street or *Mr. Kotteman* in his horse drawn wagon selling "Roman Candy."

Not too far away, at 734 South Carrollton Avenue near St. Charles Avenue, is the *River Bend*, where lots of the neighbors, including Tulane, Loyola, and Newcomb students, eat a full meal. For a lighter snack, nearer the river there's the *Camellia Grill* (626 South Carrollton Avenue), where Harry Tervalon holds forth, at the counter, serving a great hamburger and other foods, along with his expertise on Yankee baseball stats. He can't be stumped!

For a real summer treat, try *Hansen's Sno-Bliz* (4801 Tchoupitoulas Street)—a cup full of shaved ice flavored with your choice of a myriad of home-made syrups. If you're real hot and thirsty, you can buy a $200.00 pail!

A ride on Magazine Street to 4330 lands you at *Casamento's* (closed July and August) where you can find an "Oyster Loaf," a full loaf of unsliced white bread. The crust is trimmed on all six sides—the loaf is then opened up, toasted, buttered, and filled with delicious fried oysters, garnished to taste.

Continue toward the French Quarter, and stop at *Cafe Achafalaya* (901 Louisiana Avenue) so you can "Pincha-da-tail and Sucka-dahead" which is our way of teaching you to eat hot, boiled crawfish. Also available are baskets of boiled shrimp and trays of hot, boiled crabs.

In the French Quarter it's worth seeking out the *Central Grocery* (923 Decatur Street) for Muffaletta Sandwiches with salami, ham, provoloni cheese, relish, olives, pimiento, anchovies, and on and on. Half a sandwich is all you can manage.

La Madeleine (547 St. Ann Street) and *La Marquise* (625 Chartres Street), both near Jackson Square, are wonderful French bakeries which also serve croissant sandwiches.

In the block behind D. H. Holmes department store is Holmes' *Out Back Deli* (corner of Dauphine and Iberville Streets). Almost anything from Scotch salmon to super Cajun-Creole food is served.

Down Iberville Street one block is the *Acme Oyster Bar* (724 Iberville Street) where the shuckers are standing ready to open oysters for you to eat fresh from the shell. Many devotees claim the Acme has its own oyster beds.

Pepper jelly (ask "Buddy" at *Langenstein's*, 1330 Arabella Street) is often used in New Orleans as an hors d'oeuvre. It may be served with cheese, smoked duck, pork chops, ham, or any cold "left-over" meat. It will tickle your palate.

Tasso, andouille, boudin, and other Cajun sausages are some of the items found in New Orleans at *Creole Country* (512 David Street).

ENJOY!

ABOUT THE AUTHOR

Phyllis Dennery is the founder of La Fête, the New Orleans Food and Cookery Celebration. She served as President of WYES, the New Orleans Public Television Station, as a member of the Louisiana State Public Broadcasting Board, and as a member of the board of the Public Broadcasting Service—P.B.S.—as well as a member of the board of the New Orleans Public Radio Station.

Mrs. Dennery was a national individual winner of the National Volunteer Association's award in 1978, being recognized for her efforts in getting Congress to adopt the "Dennery Amendment" to the Communications Act, recognizing volunteer contributions to public broadcasting. She is a member of the Advisory Board of the New Orleans Museum of Art and a member of the Louisiana State Museum Board.

RECIPE INDEX

RECIPE INDEX

Drinks

Entrées

Salad Dressing

Salads

RECIPE INDEX

Sauces

Seasoning

Soups

Stocks

Vegetables

DINING IN-WITH THE GREAT CHEFS
A Collection of Gourmet Recipes from the Finest Chefs in the Country

Each book contains gourmet recipes for complete meals from the chefs of 21 great restaurants.

____ *Dining In–Baltimore* $7.95	____ *Dining In–Monterey Peninsula* 7.95
____ *Dining In–Boston (Revised)* 8.95	____ *Dining In–Napa Valley* 8.95
____ *Dining In–Chicago, Vol. III* 8.95	____ *Dining In–New Orleans* 8.95
____ *Dining In–Cleveland* 8.95	____ *Dining In–Philadelphia* 8.95
____ *Dining In–Dallas (Revised)* 8.95	____ *Dining In–Phoenix* 8.95
____ *Dining In–Denver* 7.95	____ *Dining In–Pittsburgh (Revised)* 7.95
____ *Dining In–Hampton Roads* 8.95	____ *Dining In–Portland* 7.95
____ *Dining In–Hawaii* 7.95	____ *Dining In–St. Louis* 7.95
____ *Dining In–Houston, Vol. II* 7.95	____ *Dining In–Salt Lake City* 8.95
____ *Dining In–Kansas City (Revised)* 7.95	____ *Dining In–San Francisco, Vol II* 7.95
____ *Dining In–Los Angeles (Revised)* 8.95	____ *Dining In–Seattle* 8.95
____ *Dining In–Manhattan* 8.95	____ *Dining In–Sun Valley* 7.95
____ *Dining In–Miami* 8.95	____ *Dining In–Toronto* 7.95
____ *Dining In–Milwaukee* 7.95	____ *Dining In–Vancouver, B.C.* 8.95
____ *Dining In–Minneapolis/St. Paul, Vol. II* . . $8.95	____ *Dining In–Washington, D.C.* 8.95

☐ Check (✔) here if you would like to have a different Dining In–Cookbook sent to you once a month. Payable by MasterCard or VISA. Returnable if not satisfied.

☐ Payment enclosed $_____ (Please include $1.00 postage and handling for each book)

☐ Charge to:

Visa # _____ Exp. Date _____

MasterCard # _____ Exp. Date _____

Signature _____

Name _____

Address _____

City _____ State _____ Zip _____

SHIP TO (if other than name and address above):

Name _____

Address _____

City _____ State _____ Zip _____

PEANUT BUTTER PUBLISHING
329 - 2nd Avenue W. ▪ Seattle, WA 98119 ▪ (206) 281-5965

DNO1085